Advancing the Mission of the Church

Best Practices in Stewardship and Development for Catholic Organizations

Advancing
the Mission
of the Church

Best Practices in Stewardship and Development
for Catholic Organizations

DANIEL CONWAY

O'MEARA,
FERGUSON,
WHELAN,
AND CONWAY

Saint Catherine of Siena Press
Indianapolis

Saint Catherine of Siena Press
4812 North Park Avenue
Indianapolis, IN 46205
888-232-1492
www.saintcathpress.com
www.omearaferguson.com

To order additional copies of this book or other publications by Daniel Conway, contact Theological Book Service at 877-484-1600 or log onto www.theobooks.org

Printed in the United States of America.

ISBN-13: 978-0-9800284-1-6

Library of Congress Control Number: 2009924742

Front cover photograph of the Cathedral of Christ the Light, Oakland, California, by Andrew Sherman of San Francisco.

Front and back cover design and interior layout by Mark Castillo.

Back cover photograph of Daniel Conway by Michael Wayne Walker, Portraits of Distinction, Plano, Texas

Dedication

This collection of essays is dedicated to the memories of my four mentors who are now deceased:

John S. MacCauley, former vice president for development,
Saint Meinrad Archabbey and Seminary

Fr. Paul Reinert, S.J., former president and chancellor,
St. Louis University

Henry A. Rosso, founder and former director,
The Fund Raising School

Most Rev. Thomas J. Murphy,
former archbishop of Seattle and
chairman of the U.S. bishops' ad hoc committee on stewardship

They believed in, and taught, the importance of development, the ministry of fundraising, the joy of giving and the spirituality of stewardship. May their witness continue to advance the mission of the Church for generations to come.

Table of Contents

Introduction

I agree with Dan Conway that the idea of advancing the mission of the Church is often misunderstood or it is not understood at all. As he logs his considerable experience of more than three decades in the field of development and Christian stewardship, he provides a truly helpful handbook for understanding the relationship of advancement and the mission of the Church. But this is not a technical handbook about how to raise money.

I know from my 30-some years' association with Dan Conway that he is at the top of professionals in the field of stewardship and development in the Catholic Church in the United States. He knows how to integrate principles of Christian stewardship with the practice of professional fundraising. He is at once an alert lay theologian, an excellent writer and communicator, and a man of deep faith.

What distinguishes development or advancement of a Catholic diocese, parish, or school? Dan's response is clear: It is the deliberate focus on the mission of the Church that is both divine and human. He reminds us insistently that the *end* of mission advancement is the successful engagement of clergy, religious and members of Christ's faithful in articulating the mission and pursuing the pastoral priorities of the Church. Advancement and fundraising serve the Catholic mission, not vice versa.

The mission of the Church is to proclaim and establish the Kingdom of God among all people. Dan Conway asks: "How many Catholics understand this mission?" His work is a veritable roadmap to help bishops and other leaders of the Church "promote unity that does not yet exist for the sake of a mission that is just beginning to be realized." He provides a vision and a practical guide for bishops and other pastoral leaders in the work of pastoral planning and leading a team in mission advancement. He makes a compelling case that mission advancement is a significant aid in evangelization.

Dan repeatedly points to the U.S. bishops' 1992 pastoral letter, *Stewardship: A Disciple's Response.* He underscores the thesis that stewardship and mission advancement are intimately related through the teaching and practice of Christian discipleship.

This book is a good read and delivers on the promise of its title. It is a unique and important account of best practices in stewardship and development for Catholic dioceses and organizations.

Most Rev. Daniel M. Buechlein, O.S.B.
Archbishop of Indianapolis

This little book of reflections on *Advancing the Mission of the Church: Best Practices in Stewardship and Development for Catholic Organizations* is the result of my more than 30 years' experience in a profession that is frequently misunderstood. Even the name of this profession is controversial. I choose to call it "mission advancement," but it is also called "development" (or "stewardship and development"), "institutional advancement" or just plain "fundraising." Most people have a very limited concept of what a "director of development" does. They know it has something to do with raising money—not something most people understand or approve of, especially in the Church. But how one becomes a development director or carries out this profession on a daily basis is a mystery to nearly everyone including those Church leaders who have to hire professional fundraisers, and work closely with them, in order to obtain the human and financial resources needed to carry out the Church's mission.

The concepts discussed here are part of a legacy, a body of professional knowledge and experience, that was handed on to me by some remarkably gifted people who served with distinction in this frequently misunderstood area of the Church's ministry. I have tried to practice what I learned from them, my mentors in the field of mission advancement, and to reflect on it and share it with others. My personal "mission-advancement story" is included at the end of this collection of essays, and in it I try to acknowledge the key figures who influenced me in my earliest years as a development officer, a fundraising professional and a stewardship educator.

The legacy I received from my mentors has been tested, and validated, in my own experience—first as a student working in a development office, then as a staff member and chief development officer in a Catholic seminary and in three archdioceses, and, now, as a full-time teacher, writer and consultant who has worked with dozens of dioceses, religious communities and seminaries in the areas of planning, stewardship education and fundraising. My hope is that these reflections will help carry forward this body of knowledge and experience and, in the process, help others understand and practice what it takes to advance the mission of the Church in a professional and faith-filled way.

After more than three decades, I know that my professional calling— my life's work—is **to help the Church integrate principles of Christian stewardship with the practice of professional fundraising.** The means to this end is what I call "mission advancement," a series of processes or techniques that can help bishops, pastors, religious superiors and other Church leaders develop the resources they need to advance the Church's mission and, in so doing, to continue Christ's work of teaching, healing and sanctifying all God's people here and now.

As I reflect on my experience in the field of mission advancement, it's my hope that these essays will help clarify basic principles and describe some of the "best practices" that make-up a successful mission-advancement program in a diocese, religious community, parish, school or other Catholic organization. I describe this book as a collection of essays because I have not attempted to write a systematic treatment (from A to Z) of everything that could be said about this subject. That would require a much longer book—one that busy people might purchase out of curiosity and then set aside. My hope is that each chapter in this collection can stand alone as a reflection on a particular aspect of the overall topic that is mission advancement, allowing readers to pick and choose. This means that there will inevitably be some repetition of material from one chapter to the next. I hope that this repetition is not distracting. I mean it to provide emphasis and to stimulate reflection.

With this in mind, please consider this a "pick-up-put-down-pick-up book" rather than one to be read straight through. And, as you prepare to read some or all of these essays on mission advancement, I invite you to think about your own understanding and experience of the fundamental concepts that will be explored in some detail in this book. Specifically, I invite you to ask yourself: What do the terms *stewardship, development, mission advancement and fundraising* mean? What do these concepts have in common? What separates or distinguishes them? What is the role of a bishop, religious superior, pastor or other Church leader in each of these activities? What roles do leadership groups (consultative bodies, boards or councils) play in each of these functions? What about key administrators and staff members? What about volunteers?

As I share some of my experiences working in this frequently misunderstood area of Church life, it's my hope that I can provide some helpful insights into all these questions.

Above all, I hope that these reflections on the opportunities and challenges of mission advancement will help Church leaders teach stewardship as a way of life and, in the process, develop the human and financial resources that are essential to carrying out Christ's work.

Daniel Conway
Solemnity of All Saints
Rome, Italy
November 1, 2008

Defining our terms

The essays in this book of reflections on mission advancement use terms that are often confused. With this in mind, it's important for me to define, and distinguish, four different but related terms: *stewardship, philanthropy, development* (or *advancement*) and *fundraising*. All these concepts, as I understand them, have a role to play in advancing the Church's mission. It's my hope that the definitions below, although certainly not exhaustive, will help clarify what these terms mean and how they are related to, and distinguished from, one another in the work of mission advancement.

1. Stewardship

Stewardship is a grateful response in faith to the Lord's invitation, "Go, sell what you have; give to the poor... and come, follow me" (Mk 10:21). Stewardship is an expression of Christian discipleship, a practical form of spirituality. It is faith in action. Stewardship can be defined as an attitude of the mind and heart that is expressed in action. It is not a program, a fundraiser, a technique for increasing volunteers or the weekly collection.

As the U.S. bishops tell us in their 1992 pastoral letter, *Stewardship: A Disciple's Response,* a Christian steward is someone who is grateful, responsible, generous and willing to give back to God with increase. Christian stewards acknowledge God as the owner and giver of all that we have and are as human beings, children of God, brothers and sisters to each other, and guardians or caretakers of all God's creation. A good steward *takes care of* and *shares* all God's gifts.

Stewardship is an integral part of mission advancement because disciples of Jesus Christ are called to carry forward the Church's mission. We have been given the "great commission" to go out to the whole world and proclaim the good news in the name of the Father, the Son and the Holy Spirit. We are personally committed, through our baptism, to be missionaries for Christ—in our homes, our work places, our neighborhoods and communities, our parishes, our schools and our dioceses. Good stewards advance the mission of the Church through their personal witness to Christ; through their active participation in the Church's ministries of worship, evangelization and faith formation; and through their service to all who are in need.

2. Philanthropy

The word *philanthropy* comes from the Greek term for "love of humanity." It is also an attitude of the mind and heart expressed in action.

Professor Robert Payton of the Center on Philanthropy at Indiana University defines philanthropy as "voluntary action for the public good." Philanthropy is any action freely undertaken for the betterment of human society. It is not just something for wealthy elites. *Any* voluntary action carried out by *anyone* (rich or poor, famous or unknown) for the benefit of human society can be a philanthropic activity. That would include barn raisings by neighboring farmers, walk-a-thons sponsored by civic groups, Three Tenors or rock concerts, homebuilding activities sponsored by Habitat for Humanity or neighbors helping neighbors.

What's the difference between stewardship and philanthropy? Stewardship is a personal faith response to the equally personal invitation each of us has received from Jesus Christ to be his disciple. Philanthropy is a more generic response to humanitarian, cultural or social needs. Both require gratitude, responsibility, generosity and the willingness to give back. As the Roman orator Cicero once said, "Gratitude is not only the greatest of virtues; it is the parent of all the others." Contemporary research shows that there is an important correlation between gratitude and health (mental, emotional and physical). Grateful sharing and giving back is good for individuals and for society!

3. Development/Advancement

Development (or institutional advancement) refers to a program of planned or systematic growth. Whether we are talking about human development, spiritual development or resource development, we have in mind processes that signify movement, growth or advancement from a certain point in time and space to a new, and hopefully desired, future.

It is said that the term *development office* or *development department* was first used in Chicago in the 1920s at two distinguished universities—The University of Chicago and Northwestern University. The objective of these universities' development departments was to tie fundraising activities that were threatening to become ends in themselves (or "the tail wagging the dog") to the university's academic blueprint—its vision and plan for the future. In other words, the goal was to link fundraising with the mission and priorities of the university. To accomplish this significant change in the way fundraising was carried out—making it integral to accomplishing the university's mission rather than regarding it as the dirty work that had to be done in order to pay the bills (a "necessary evil")—several things became necessary. Here is a list of 10 things that came to be regarded as essential features of a successful development program:

- a vision—your desired future
- a plan—to realize your vision
- engaged leaders—board, executive and staff
- advocates—people of influence (and affluence) who will speak on your behalf
- strong relationships with supportive constituencies
- a compelling case for support

- excellent communications
- quality programs that make a difference in people's lives
- a commitment to the best practices of professional fundraising
- transparency and accountability in decision-making and finances—sometimes referred to as "stewardship" in the narrow sense of taking care of donors' investments in your mission.

Organizations that perform all, or most, of these essential development functions well are successful at developing the human and financial resources needed to carry out, and grow, their missions.

4. Fundraising

There are basically two kinds of fundraising: indirect and direct.

Indirect fundraising is very familiar to us in the Church. Bingo, bake sales, Monte Carlo nights, raffles, festivals, chocolate bars, used-book sales, car washes, golf tournaments, and the list goes on... . I call these "indirect" fundraising activities because the activities themselves are not directly related to the mission or services of the organization raising funds. You don't have to care about Catholic education to buy a chocolate bar or a magazine subscription.

Indirect fundraisers are low-cost, low-yield, time- and volunteer-intensive activities. In the days when most Catholics were immigrants or rural poor and personnel costs were heavily subsidized by religious orders and clergy, and when physical plants were new, our fundraising needs were generally met by these kinds of indirect fundraising activities. If everyone gave a little, we could raise enough extra money to meet the extraordinary funding needs of parishes, schools and other Catholic organizations.

Now, when our most significant costs—the people who do the Church's work, and the maintenance and updating of our facilities—can no longer be subsidized by Sisters, Brothers and priests, old methods of indirect fundraising no longer do the job. How many chocolate bars would you have to sell to provide one teacher's salary or significant tuition assistance to just one family? How many raffle tickets does it take to staff a youth ministry program for one year? To meet today's significant funding needs, you need a more comprehensive approach.

Direct fundraising asks people to participate directly in the mission of the Church—to make sacrificial gifts of time, talent and treasure to support the ministries that are being funded by this particular fundraising effort. It's no longer good enough to like chocolate or have a dirty car that needs washing. Direct fundraising asks you to care about the cause you are being asked to invest in. In a diocesan annual appeal or a parish capital campaign or a planned gifts initiative to endow a school's tuition assistance program, the more people understand and "own" the cause they are being asked to support, the more likely they are to make gifts of substance. And the more people are motivated by a genuine spirit of philanthropy or Christian stewardship, the more likely they are to share generously and to invest their personal, spiritual and financial gifts in helping to make your vision a reality.

Every professional fundraising activity—whether undertaken by a small rural parish or a large Catholic organization like the University of Notre Dame—can be characterized in terms of three essential functions:

- Finding people who share your values (prospect research)
- Building strong relationships (communications and buy-in)
- Providing diverse opportunities for engagement and investment that are appropriate to the interests and abilities of the donor (funding vehicles).

Whether your fundraising activity is run by a large professional staff or a small group of dedicated volunteer advocates, success will be measured by the quality of your efforts to carry out these three essential functions. Without the right prospects, your communications fall on deaf ears. Without first building strong relations and securing the personal engagement of your donor prospects, you will end up asking too soon and receiving a token gift rather than a gift of substance. And if you are unable to take advantage of the full range of fundraising vehicles to match the donor's needs and interests with the ministry needs you are trying to fund, you will miss key opportunities and leave lots of money "on the table."

Direct fundraising requires a professional approach that includes leadership, vision and a commitment to reach out to others and invite their ownership and investment in your mission. Indirect, or amateur, fundraising can be done by anyone anytime there is a good cause that is worthy of people's indirect support. There is nothing wrong with indirect fundraising so long as you understand its purposes and its limits, but mission advancement requires a more professional approach.

In my experience, authentic and successful mission advancement requires both indirect and direct fundraising. It requires community-building, awareness and friend-raising activities like the Bishop's Dinner for Seminarians or the Salute to Catholic School Graduates or the Parish Festival. It also requires intense prospect research, relationship-building and personal invitations to make gifts of substance to support your mission.

These are the definitions used in the essays that follow. I hope it's clear that these concepts are not contradictory or mutually exclusive. In fact, all four concepts—stewardship, philanthropy, development and fundraising—contribute to a successful mission-advancement program.

Questions for reflection and discussion

- Who is a Christian steward? What's the relationship between stewardship and discipleship?

- How are stewardship and philanthropy similar? How are they different?

- What are the essential functions of a successful development or advancement program?

- What's the difference between indirect and direct fundraising? Why is this distinction important?

❧ Prayer ❧

God of love and mercy, you call us to be faithful disciples of your son, Jesus Christ, and good stewards of all creation.

Grant us the grace to understand, and accept, the challenges and opportunities we have been given to advance the mission of your Church.

We believe that you have given us everything we need to carry out your will. Help us be steadfast in faith, confident in hope and generous in charity. That in all things you may be glorified. Amen.

Stewardship

A Christian steward is one who receives God's gifts gratefully, cherishes and tends them in a responsible and accountable manner, shares them generously in justice and love with others, and returns them with increase to the Lord (U.S. BISHOPS' 1992 PASTORAL LETTER, *STEWARDSHIP: A DISCIPLE'S RESPONSE,* P. 9).

1. How does the U.S. bishops' pastoral letter define stewardship?

Stewardship is a way of life, a practical form of spirituality. Once again, it is a response to the Lord's call to discipleship. Christian stewards are: 1) grateful for all God's gifts, 2) accountable for their development and use, 3) generous in sharing with others, and 4) willing to give back to God with increase. In *Stewardship: A Disciple's Response (SDR)*, the American bishops describe the opportunities and challenges facing all Catholic parishes and dioceses. The pastoral letter speaks of three convictions, or principles, that are at the heart of Christian stewardship.

The first conviction is that "mature disciples make a conscious, firm decision, carried out in action, to be followers of Jesus Christ no matter the cost to themselves" (*SDR*, p 5). Mature discipleship is not impulsive or short-lived. It is carefully considered, deliberately chosen and lived day-in and day-out in the concrete circumstances of our lives. With this first conviction, the bishops make it clear that stewardship is serious business. It is a way of life that is only undertaken by mature men and women who can accept the risks and who are willing to pay the price.

The second conviction is that "beginning in conversion, change of mind and heart, this commitment is expressed not in a single action, nor even a number of actions over a period of time, but in an entire way of life. It means committing one's very self to the Lord" (*SDR*, p. 5). Stewardship requires a radical change of attitude and lifestyle. It is not something that can be accomplished once and for all, but requires a lifelong commitment. And what is committed is not something incidental or extra. Stewardship demands a total commitment—heart and mind, body and soul, intentions and actions. Indeed, stewardship means committing one's very self to the Lord!

The third conviction of the U.S. bishops' pastoral letter is that "stewardship is an expression of Christian discipleship with the power to change how we understand and live our lives" (*SDR*, p. 5). It is not enough to make a conscious decision to become a disciple of Jesus Christ. It's not enough to make a total commitment of ourselves to a new way of life. *We must actually change*. We must begin to see things differently. We must change our understanding and awareness of God, of the world around us and of the people we cohabitate with on the planet Earth (including our families, our neighbors and friends, our fellow citizens, and even strangers and enemies). Above all, we must live differently and make new choices about developing and sharing all the gifts God has given us.

Stewardship is an entire way of life, an ongoing process, a journey that will last until the Day of Judgment, the day when we will all be asked to render an account of our guardianship of all God's gifts—spiritual and material. None of us can ever be perfect stewards, but we can grow in our understanding and practice of stewardship principles. We can grow as stewards. As individuals and as faith communities, we can make progress on the stewardship journey.

2. What difference does stewardship make in the lives of Christian disciples?

How do we chart our progress or measure our growth as stewards? How can we tell that our commitment to stewardship is making a difference?

Not by ordinary means. What the world considers successful—wealth, celebrity, power—can never be our standards of measurement. And yet, it is extremely difficult to step outside the cultural currents that seem to propel us all in the direction of economic, social or political acceptability. We are told incessantly that the truly successful person has a six-figure income, wears the right clothes and belongs to the right groups. Or that he or she wants desperately to have more money, to acquire more and more things and to belong to the in-crowd. We measure our success by the standards of Hollywood, Wall Street and Washington. Unless we have, or are, what others tell us are the indicators of success (the best, the latest or the most sophisticated), we feel like failures—people who somehow don't quite measure up.

In fact, the only valid measure of our success is found in *Stewardship: A Disciple's Response*. The bishops describe a Christian steward as "one who receives God's gifts gratefully, cherishes and tends them in a responsible and accountable manner, shares them generously with others out of justice and love, and returns them with increase to the Lord" (*SDR*, p. 9). These four characteristics of a Christian steward are the "benchmarks" of stewardship success. To measure our success, and our growth as stewards, we must ask ourselves:

1.   Are we more grateful (as individuals, families or communities) than we were when we first began to practice stewardship as a way of life? Have we matured in our celebration of the Eucharist? Do we thank God daily for all his gifts? Do we pray more often? Do we say "thank you" more often—to God and to the people with whom we live and work? Do we complain less? Criticize less? Covet others' possessions less? Are we more grateful for who we are and what we have than we used to be?

2.   Are we more accountable today than we were when we began to practice the principles of Christian stewardship? Do we admit our mistakes and try to learn from them? Do we cele-

brate the sacrament of penance and reconciliation regularly? Have we accepted our baptismal responsibility for the evangelical mission of the Church? Do we reach out to others through hospitality and through solidarity with the poor and with all who are in need?

3. Are we more generous? Have we grown in our willingness to share our time? Our personal gifts and talents? Our financial resources? Can we honestly say that as individuals and communities we are warmer, more caring and more generous now that we have committed ourselves to stewardship as a way of life? Are we giving what's left over—or are we sharing our very best, giving sacrificially the "first fruits" of all that we have and all that we are?

4. Finally, have we taken the gifts and talents that God has given us and helped them to grow, or have we buried them out of ignorance, apathy or fear? Have we brought out the best in ourselves and our parish and diocesan communities using all our gifts to develop and grow the Church's mission? Can we honestly say that we are growing in holiness? In prayerfulness? In our service to others? Do we gather at the altar to return God's gifts with increase?

These are the only true measures of growth in stewardship—and the only genuinely effective benchmarks of what it means to be a "stewardship" family, parish or diocese: a community of faith that is on the road to stewardship as a way of life.

3. How does stewardship as a practical form of spirituality influence the efforts of dioceses, parishes, religious communities, schools and other Catholic organizations to advance the mission of the Church?

Stewardship is not a program or a fundraising technique. It is a way of life that demands conversion—prompted by a keen awareness that everything we have, spiritual and material, is a free gift of a good and gracious God.

But it is also true that people who have accepted stewardship as a way of life are grateful and generous. And they long to become more intimately involved in carrying out the mission of the Church. In our culture, which is characterized by affluence and consumerism, a commitment to stewardship is a necessary first step in the journey to holiness. For this reason, Catholic organizations that seek to develop the human and financial resources needed to carry out Christ's work must look to stewardship not as a program or technique but as a unique means of education and formation in discipleship. Stewardship cultivates a sense of responsibility, and Catholics who accept responsibility for the Church's mission and ministries share generously of their time, talent and financial resources.

What, then, is the relationship between mission advancement and stewardship? Rightly understood, the practice of Christian stewardship helps Catholics become more aware of their own giftedness and of their responsibility to share in the Church's mission. A truly effective mission-advancement program must be built on principles of Christian stewardship. It must reinforce themes of gratitude, accountability, generous sharing and the willingness to give back to the Lord with increase.

In Catholic organizations, successful mission-advancement programs teach stewardship as a way of life. But they also model good stewardship—not just in the way they treat donors or handle gifts (although this kind of accountability is critically important). Catholic organizations are true witnesses to stewardship when they acknowledge in all humility and truth that they truly don't own or control anything but rely entirely on the grace of God who has given them a unique stewardship responsibility for human and financial resources that belong to God alone.

Mission-advancement programs that are stewardship-based do not have to apologize for employing the best practices of nonprofit management and professional fundraising. As long as the "end" is to advance the Church's mission and the "means" are consistent with stewardship as a way of life, the pastoral letter on stewardship encourages Church institutions to observe "the most stringent ethical, fiscal and legal standards" and to take full advantage of proven principles and techniques of institutional (or mission) advancement.

A truly effective mission-advancement program includes stewardship education. It also provides the Catholic people with concrete opportunities to share their gifts with others and to participate directly in the mission and ministries of the Church. It's often said that the days are past when Catholics gave simply out of a sense of obligation. Let's hope that Catholics will increasingly accept their responsibility (obligation) to give out of a profound sense of gratitude to God for all his blessings and out of a genuine desire to share all God's gifts with others out of a keen sense of justice and love. A mission-advancement program that combines stewardship education with concrete opportunities to share generously all God's gifts is truly advancing the Church's mission—through the grace of the Holy Spirit!

4. What is the relationship between mission advancement and stewardship?

Much confusion exists in the minds of Catholics, including many Church leaders, about what stewardship is and about how it relates to discipleship (the experience of daily Christian living) and the administration and funding of parishes, schools, dioceses and other Catholic institutions. To define stewardship—simply and clearly—has to be the first step in any discussion of the relationship between mission advancement and stewardship. As we seek to define stewardship for individual Christian disciples, we will find that the "spirituality of stewardship" also has implications for Catholic organizations and for the advancement of the Church's mission.

Stewardship is a response in faith to the Lord's invitation, "Go, sell what you have; give to the poor … and come, follow me" (Mk 10:21). Stewardship is an expression of Christian discipleship, a practical form of spirituality. It is faith in action. Stewardship can be defined as an attitude of the mind and heart that is expressed in action. It is not a program, a fundraiser, or a gimmick for increasing volunteers or the weekly collection.

As the U.S. bishops tell us in their pastoral letter, *Stewardship: A Disciple's Response,* a Christian steward is someone who is grateful, responsible, generous and willing to give back to God with increase. Christian stewards acknowledge God as the owner and giver of all that we have and are as human beings, children of God, brothers and sisters to each other, and guardians or caretakers of all God's creation. A good steward *takes care of* and *shares* all God's gifts.

Stewardship is an integral part of mission advancement because disciples of Jesus Christ are called to carry forward the Church's mission. We have been given the "great commission" to go out to the whole world and proclaim the good news in the name of the Father, the Son and the Holy Spirit. We are personally committed, through our baptism, to be missionaries for Christ—in our homes, our workplaces, our neighborhoods and communities, our parishes, our schools and our dioceses. Good stewards advance the mission of the Church through their personal witness to Christ, in their active participation in the Church's ministries of worship, evangelization and faith formation and in service to all who are in need.

Christians are stewards of the Body of Christ, the Church. As stewards, we are called to accept gratefully the gift of faith that is given to us in baptism. We are invited, and challenged, to nurture this gift and to allow it to grow and mature through our prayer, our participation in the Eucharist and all the sacraments, our solidarity with other Christians and with all members of the human family (especially the poor and vulnerable), and our faithful observance of Church teaching. As disciples of Jesus Christ, and stewards of his body, we are called to share generously with others all the spiritual and material blessings we have received from a good and gracious God. Finally, our mission as stewards is to grow all the gifts God has given us so that we can "give them back with increase" on the Last Day.

How do we "advance" the mission that we have received from Christ as his faithful disciples? Isn't this the work of the Holy Spirit—to guide the Church in the exercise of her divine mission and to ensure that the resources needed to carry out this mission are provided? Surely this is a responsibility that far exceeds the abilities of even the most dedicated professionals, whether clergy or lay, who are charged with administrative responsibilities in the areas of planning, communications, stewardship education and fundraising.

To advance the mission of the Church, we must rely—first and foremost—on God's grace. Proclamation of the Word, celebration of the sacraments, the ministry of charity and the building up of Christ's Kingdom do not happen because of our efforts at "mission advancement." They happen because the Holy Spirit is active in the Church, and in us, calling forth the gifts of vocation, of faith sharing and of service that are needed to develop and grow the Body of Christ. We engage in mission advancement as disciples who have been called to participate in the mission of the Church and who have accepted the responsibility to serve as stewards (guardians or caretakers) of work that properly belongs to our Divine Master, the one who has entrusted to our care his ministry of hope and salvation for all.

As we are using the term here, *advancement* is a systematic and comprehensive process that requires leadership, a supporting constituency and resources (human, physical and financial). Advancement is the means to an end (the mission of the Church), not an end in itself. It is a way of helping dioceses, parishes, religious communities, schools and other Catholic organizations develop the human and financial resources they need to carry out Christ's work.

To understand the role of stewardship in mission advancement we must ask the following questions: What is the mission of a diocese, parish, religious community, school or other Catholic organization as an agency of the Church? How do we participate in the mission of the Universal Church? How does our work contribute to the advancement of the Church's divine and human mission? Do we have a vision for the future? What are our priorities? What are our most significant resource needs? Do we have the leadership, relationships and discipline needed to develop the resources that are needed to advance our particular mission as well as the mission of the Church Universal?

And, then, we must ask: What is the role of stewardship in all this? Is it integral to the process of advancing our particular mission and the mission of the larger Church? Or is stewardship something altogether different and unrelated?

Stewardship plays a critical role in our efforts to advance the Church's mission. Regardless of whether we use the terms *stewardship, development* or *advancement,* to carry forward the mission of the Church, we must help Catholics reflect on the ways they have been gifted by God. And we must invite, and challenge, them to share generously with others all the spiritual and material gifts they have received. Catholic communities that practice stewardship as a way of life are grateful, responsible, generous and eager to give back to the Lord with increase. They are communities dedicated to advancing the mission of the Church through evangelization, faith formation and the ministry of charity. Stewardship and mission advancement are not the same thing. But they are intimately related through the teaching and practice of Christian discipleship.

Techniques of stewardship education and mission advancement must always be recognized as secondary to the far more fundamental task of proclaiming the Kingdom of God (evangelization) and giving witness to the person of Jesus Christ (discipleship). It is the Holy Spirit's job to advance the mission of the Church. We are privileged to participate in this divine mission as stewards of the Body of Christ committed to developing the human, physical and financial resources that are needed to carry out Christ's work.

Questions for reflection and discussion

1. How does the U.S. bishops' pastoral letter define stewardship?

2. What difference does stewardship make in the daily lives of Christian disciples?

3. How does stewardship as a practical form of spirituality influence the efforts of dioceses, parishes, religious communities, schools and other Catholic organizations to advance the mission of the Church?

4. What is the relationship between mission advancement and stewardship?

❧ **Prayer** ❧

All powerful and ever-living God, we do well always and everywhere to give you thanks. All things are of your making. All times and seasons obey you.

You chose to create us in your own image and to set us over the whole world in all its wonder. You made us stewards of creation, to praise you every day for your wisdom and power.

May we imitate your son, Jesus Christ, in his prayer, his teaching and his life of service. May we be faithful stewards of all your gifts to us, the one family of God. Amen.

Mission Advancement

Henceforward the Church, endowed with the gifts of her founder and faithfully observing his precepts of charity, humility and self-denial, receives the mission of proclaiming and establishing among all peoples the kingdom of Christ and of God, and she is, on earth, the seed and the beginning of that kingdom. While she slowly grows to maturity, the Church longs for the completed kingdom and, with all her strength, hopes and desires to be united in glory with her king (LUMEN GENTIUM, THE DOGMATIC CONSTITUTION ON THE CHURCH, #5).

1. What is mission advancement?

The term *mission advancement* refers to a comprehensive, systematic process designed to carry forward the mission of the Church in a diocese, parish, religious community, school or other Catholic organization. This concept is clearly related to *development* and *institutional advancement* as they are used by various kinds of nonprofit organizations both faith-based and secular. What distinguishes development or advancement in the case of a Catholic organization is its deliberate focus on the mission of the Church, which is both divine and human and which is paradoxically both similar to and completely different from other kinds of organizations that seek to develop or advance their missions.

What is similar to all other organizations?

Successful advancement requires strong leadership, excellent communications and a well-managed organization with an effective fundraising program.

What's different?

Although Catholic organizations use principles and techniques of financial management, personnel administration and professional fundraising to develop and manage the temporal resources that are essential for ministry, in the final analysis, the Church's mission extends beyond the practical day-to-day realities of institutional life to a realm that is profoundly spiritual. This all-important dimension of mystery (the sacramental nature of the Church) should never be an excuse for poor stewardship of the Church's resources. But it does require us to "look deeper" when we talk about our vision for the future and to attend to the special character of the Church as the Body of Christ when we formulate strategies and action plans for carrying out Christ's work in the world today.

Mission advancement requires the active leadership and support of the bishop, pastor, religious superior or chief administrator who is charged with the responsibility for expressing a clear sense of mission and priorities, building strong relationships with the people whose help is needed to carry out the organization's mission, and developing the human, physical and financial resources that are needed to make the organization's vision and plans for the future a reality.

Through the *means* of mission advancement, the organization's leaders are provided with instruments for developing and implementing 1) statements of vision and mission tailored to particular needs and circumstances, 2) a pastoral plan and priorities, 3) strategies for successful communication of the organization's plans, and 4) principles and techniques for building the organization's capacity to develop the human and financial resources needed to carry out the mission of the Church. The *end* of this comprehensive process of advancement is the successful engagement of clergy, religious and members of Christ's faithful in the mission and pastoral priorities of the Church so that their individual and combined gifts of time, talent and treasure can carry forward the organization's distinctive mission.

What are the signs of a successful mission-advancement program in a diocese, parish, religious community, school or other Catholic organization?

- Strong leaders with a clear sense of purpose and a plan for the future.
- Excellent communications that inform, inspire and invite clergy, religious and lay people to become engaged in the organization's work for the Church.
- Temporal resources that are well-managed and that grow in proportion to the organization's vision and priorities.

In the end, of course, a mission-advancement program is only recognized as successful when the work of the Church is carried forward. This requires spiritual vitality, evangelization, the work of charity and the human and financial resources needed to sustain Christ's work. Mission advancement is never an end in itself. It is always a means to a much more important end—proclaiming the Gospel and building up the Body of Christ.

2. What is the mission of the Church? How does "advancement" contribute to carrying out this mission?

"When Jesus, having died on the cross for men, rose again from the dead, he was seen to be constituted as Lord, the Christ, and as Priest for ever, and he poured out on his disciples the Spirit promised by the Father. Henceforward the Church, endowed with the gifts of her founder and faithfully observing his precepts of charity, humility and self-denial, receives *the mission of proclaiming and establishing among all peoples the kingdom of Christ and of God, and she is, on earth, the seed and the beginning of that kingdom.* While she slowly grows to maturity, the Church longs for the completed kingdom and, with all her strength, hopes and desires to be united in glory with her king" (*Lumen Gentium,* the Dogmatic Constitution on the Church, #5. emphasis added).

The mission of the Church is to proclaim and establish among all peoples the Kingdom of God. The Church is called to be the seed and beginning of that which she proclaims. Advancement of this mission is acknowledged to be slow and gradual, but growth in mission is carried out with a profound sense of hope and a deep longing for the day when this divine mission will be fulfilled in Christ.

The process we call mission advancement begins with understanding and a careful articulation of this received mission of the Church in the context of a particular diocese, parish, religious community, school or other Catholic organization. The Church is the same always and everywhere, but the challenges and opportunities that individual Catholic organizations face vary according to different historic, economic, political and cultural circumstances. The first step in any mission-advancement effort is to provide members of the Catholic community with opportunities to reflect on, and better understand, the Church's mission as it is expressed in the particular mission of each individual diocese, parish, religious community, school and Catholic organization. This process of raising awareness about the Church's mission is itself a part of the work of evangelization because education about the Church must always also be a proclamation of the Good News of our salvation in Christ and an invitation to accept the Lord's call to be his disciples and help transform the world in the concrete circumstances of their daily lives.

This process of "mission education" and evangelization is first and foremost the bishop's responsibility, but it is a responsibility the bishop shares with many others, including his priests and deacons, with the leaders of religious communities, with the administrators of Catholic organizations in his diocese and with all baptized Christians. So, for example, when the superior of a women's religious order invites her Sisters to reflect on and articulate their community's mission, she is participating in the larger work of evangelization by calling attention to the distinctive charisms of her community and the ways in which the members of her order contribute to the proclamation of the Gospel through their prayer, the witness of their lives and their apostolic work.

Too often, the mission of a Catholic organization is "assumed." But how many Catholics really understand what a diocese is? Or how many know why religious men and women live the way they do? Or how Catholic organizations such as schools, hospitals and social service agencies contribute to "proclaiming and establishing among all peoples the Kingdom of God?"

Mission is not something we can afford to take for granted. Mission education is the necessary first step in any successful advancement program because understanding is the key to participation and engagement. That's why planning for the future begins with a statement of mission. It's also why it's important for official communications should consistently remind Catholics of the overall mission of the Church and the ways in which dioceses, parishes, schools and other Catholic organizations participate in carrying out this mission.

Experience shows that if you help people understand what your mission is and invite them to participate through their prayers, their personal involvement and their financial support, they will give generously from the heart. On the other hand, even generous people will hold back (at some level at least) when they do not understand or do not feel a part of organizations whose purposes and accomplishments are unclear to them. Successful mission-advancement programs strive to inform, involve, inspire and invite people to participate actively in the mission and ministries of the Church.

3.   How is mission advancement different in a Catholic diocese?

There is an essential difference and some accidental ones. The essential difference between mission advancement in the Church and in other organizations stems from the nature of the Church as a sacred reality that is both divine and human. The Church is not simply an institution or a social organization that serves a noble cause (although the Church is both institutional and social and its cause is noble indeed).

The Church is the Body of Christ and the sacrament of humanity's call to perfect communion with God, and with all created reality, in and through the person of Jesus Christ. As the mission of the Church clearly indicates (cf. *Lumen Gentium,* the Dogmatic Constitution on the Church, #5), the Church is not yet what it seeks to become. The Church is the seed and beginning of the Kingdom it proclaims and seeks to establish. The Church is a pilgrim people journeying toward an as yet unrealized future. The slow and gradual growth in mission, which is part of the very nature of the Church, can cause frustration and disappointment among those who are eager to achieve perfection and see the mission fulfilled. This is not meant as an excuse for inaction or a casual attitude toward carrying out the work of Christ on earth. On the contrary, it is a reflection of the fact that much hard work and zeal for the apostolic mission of the Church are required in spite of the fact that we have no way of knowing when the end we seek, the completion of God's Kingdom, will be accomplished.

Advancing the mission of the Church is therefore a profoundly spiritual undertaking—designed to effect the transformation of individuals, and the whole of human society, into a holy people united in faith, hope and love as the one family of God. While we can make significant progress in this process of transformation, the work we are called to do as disciples of Jesus Christ will not be finally accomplished until he comes again at the end of time.

In the Church, mission advancement must be seen as more than trying to accomplish a social good (or a series of goods such as worship, faith formation, evangelization or social ministry). Mission advancement for the Church must be seen as a participation in the mystery of the Church, which is both divine and human. It must be understood as a collaboration in the work of the Holy Spirit who is "for the Church and for each and every believer, the principle of their union and unity in the teaching of the apostles and fellowship, in the breaking of the bread and prayer" (*Lumen Gentium,* the Dogmatic Constitution on the Church, #13).

Several accidental differences exist between mission advancement in the Church and in other organizations. Catholic dioceses are multifaceted organizations with a wide variety of parochial and diocesan ministries that all come under the pastoral leadership of the bishop. Mission advancement is easier to achieve in a self-contained institution (like a school) or in an organization that has one all-embracing purpose—for example, to feed the homeless or provide hospice care to the dying. A multifaceted organization like a diocese ironically has too many good things going on. So many good things, in fact, that it's difficult to communicate them all in clear, simple and compelling ways. The executive director of a local chapter of Habitat for Humanity, for example, can articulate his or her vision using examples that all reinforce the vision of providing low-cost housing for the poor. A diocesan bishop's vision may embrace this same priority—and a dozen others as well!

A Catholic diocese is a geographic unit comprising many diverse communities with significantly different cultural, racial, social and economic realities. Mission advancement is more challenging in an environment of great diversity. The bishop of a large urban diocese, for example, must address his vision to people who represent many different cultural and ethnic communities. He must speak to women and men from very different social and economic backgrounds. Finally, the bishop must reach out to people who are not necessarily of like mind on social, political and even religious issues.

All too often a Catholic diocese is regarded by its members as a purely juridical entity; in fact many Catholics would not consider their diocese to be a community they belong to by choice. Unlike a university president who addresses alumni/ae and those who are affiliated with the university by choice, the diocesan bishop must address audiences that are much more diverse and far less engaged. His task is to promote a unity that does not yet exist for the sake of a mission that is just beginning to be realized!

Finally, active participation in the work of the diocese has historically been limited to clergy, diocesan staff and a few lay leaders. The majority of Catholics, even if they regularly support the diocese's annual appeal, do not consider themselves to be significant contributors to the mission or ministries of the diocesan Church. Mission advancement seeks to change this—to encourage the active participation of all Catholics in the life of the Church at many different levels and to provide people of faith with concrete opportunities to share their gifts of time, talent and treasure with their diocesan and parish communities.

4. What is the role of the bishop in mission advancement?

The bishop's role in mission advancement coincides with his role and responsibilities as the chief teacher and pastor of the diocesan Church. The process we call mission advancement is not something separate or additional the bishop must do in order to reorganize his diocesan ministries or raise funds for their support. It is designed to help him carry out his responsibility to exercise responsible stewardship of the spiritual and temporal resources entrusted to his care. Done properly, the mission-advancement process should strengthen and support the bishop in all his efforts to teach, sanctify and provide pastoral leadership for his diocese.

Pope John Paul II has provided important guidance on the role of the bishop in mission advancement in his 2001 apostolic letter *Novo Millennio Ineunte* (At the Beginning of the New Millennium). In this remarkable document, the Holy Father persuasively argues for a form of planning that is profoundly pastoral.

According to Pope John Paul: "It is not therefore a matter of inventing a 'new program.' The program already exists: it is the plan found in the Gospel and in the living Tradition, it is the same as ever. Ultimately, it has its center in Christ himself, who is to be known, loved and imitated, so that in him we may live the life of the Trinity, and with him transform history until its fulfillment in the heavenly Jerusalem. This is a program which does not change with shifts of times and cultures, even though it takes account of time and culture for the sake of true dialogue and effective communication. This program for all times is our program for the Third Millennium. But it must be translated into *pastoral initiatives adapted to the circumstances of each community*" (#29, emphasis added).

In the context of this powerful description of the kind of pastoral planning that is appropriate (indeed, essential) to carrying forward the mission of the Church in the new millennium, it is clear that the bishop is responsible, first and foremost, for making sure that "the plan found in the Gospel and in the living Tradition" is successfully translated into a vision statement and pastoral plan that adapts the timeless and unchanging way of living, which is Jesus Christ himself, into pastoral initiatives that are adapted to the particular needs and circumstances of his diocese.

The bishop serves as the initiator and overseer of the mission-advancement process. His specific responsibilities are to:

1. Provide spiritual leadership through prayer and discernment of the Lord's will for his Church.

2. Select the leadership team (includes diocesan staff, clergy and lay volunteers) that will design and implement the process.

3. Engage as many people as is practical in formulating and communicating vision and priorities, developing and implementing a pastoral plan, setting strategies for stewardship education and resource development.

4. Participate in all of the above at key moments. Listening carefully to what others are saying but also providing guidance and direction.

5. Promulgate the vision and plan for the local Church.

6. Set priorities for the plan's implementation.

7. Approve the diocese's case for support (with detailed opportunities for investment) and make it his own—in order to communicate it effectively in various individual and small-group settings.

8. Invite gifts of time, talent and treasure—including leadership and major gifts—to fund the vision and plan.

9. Build strong relationships with contributors and encourage ongoing participation through annual giving, major gifts and planned gifts.

10. Thank all donors as personally as possible and provide opportunities to recognize and involve those who make significant gifts of time, talent or treasure to help carry out the Church's mission.

These 10 responsibilities, which characterize the bishop's role in mission advancement, would also apply to a pastor, religious superior, or the chief administrator of a Catholic school, hospital or social service agency. What is important to note is that mission advancement is not incompatible with authentic religious leadership. On the contrary, to the extent that the process we call mission advancement is true to its name, it should be a significant help to any Church leader in the exercise of his or her ministry.

5. Successful mission advancement requires a team

Many organizations make the mistake of hiring a development director (experienced or inexperienced) and expecting him or her to be solely responsible for fundraising success.

As we have defined mission advancement for Catholic organizations, it involves the coordination and integration of these essential functions: a) articulating a vision for the future, b) developing and implementing a pastoral plan, c) communicating the vision and building support for the plan, d) teaching stewardship as a way of life and encouraging all members of the Catholic community, and others as appropriate, to become personally engaged in the Church's mission and e) developing the human and financial resources needed to carry out the organization's mission and priorities.

Many dioceses have separate departments or offices that are responsible for one or more of these functions (for example, an office for pastoral planning, a communications office and a stewardship office). Other Catholic organizations may combine most or all of these functions into one office or department or include them under the aegis of a foundation that is separate from the administration or corporate control of the diocese, religious community or institution. Whatever structure is chosen, it is vitally important that the five functions listed above be carefully coordinated.

Because mission advancement is a complex process requiring many different skills and experiences, it is important for the bishop, pastor, religious superior or chief administrator to delegate various advancement functions to a diverse team of people, including staff and volunteers, who can collaborate in designing and implementing the organization's mission-advancement program.

This team will need to possess a variety of gifts and talents in order to implement successfully the essential functions of mission advancement. For example, visioning and planning require attentive listening, discernment and prudent decision-making. In addition, excellent communication skills are needed at every stage of the mission-advancement process. Collaboration and a strong sense of teamwork must be combined with a respectful acknowledgment and acceptance of the lines of authority and responsibility prescribed by Church law and local custom. Creativity and innovation should be welcomed and encouraged—provided that the team clearly understands that its role is not to "reinvent the wheel" but to adapt the program of the Gospel and of the Church's living tradition to meet the concrete needs and circumstances of a particular diocesan Church, parish, religious community, school or agency.

Each bishop, pastor, religious superior or chief administrator should choose his or her mission-advancement team based on the needs of his or her organization and its history, local culture and traditions. It is important for the team to be representative and diverse, but the primary requirement for membership on the team is the ability to think and work on behalf of the whole community. Advocacy for special interests can be helpful to the overall advancement process, but the leadership team must be a group whose main commitment is to the common good.

Most Catholic dioceses already have in place several leadership groups, including the bishop's cabinet, the diocesan curia, the priests' council, the diocesan consultors, the finance council, pastoral council and stewardship committee or foundation board—as well as other boards, commissions and committees. Religious communities and other Catholic organizations often have similar structures. As a general rule, none of these existing groups is totally responsible for all the functions that need to be coordinated in a comprehensive mission-advancement program. That's why it's important for the bishop to designate a team that includes appropriate representation from each of the organization's various boards, committees and administrative structures.

The mission-advancement leadership team is called upon to exercise three distinct functions according to the members' expertise and experience.

1. Senior members of the organization's staff are asked to help the bishop, pastor, religious superior or chief administrator in visioning and planning, especially from the perspective of their major areas of responsibility. They also have an important role to play advising on the organization's priorities and helping identify significant gift opportunities (program support, capital improvements or endowments). Finally, senior staff members can help communicate the organization's vision for the future and invite others to make substantial gifts of time, talent and treasure to carry out the organization's mission.

2. Council, board and committee members (whether clergy, religious or lay) are asked to advocate for the mission and priorities of the organization not only within their specific areas of responsibility (for example, finance council or school board) but also among the wider Catholic community and the general public. This advocacy role is vitally important to the overall advancement process because it provides a powerful independent witness to the organization's vision and priorities and to the importance of active engagement by Catholics in all aspects of the Church's mission and ministries. In addition to their role as witnesses or advocates, volunteer leaders may also be asked to assume specific duties in the overall advancement process—from plan development and implementation, to communications and leadership enlistment, to various responsibilities in resource development (for example, leadership positions in the annual appeal, major-gift development, capital campaigns or planned-giving activities).

3. Advancement staff may include directors of stewardship and development, the president or executive of a Catholic foundation, or other staff persons who have responsibilities in pastoral planning, communications or fundraising for the organization. What all of these positions have in common is the responsibility to manage all or any part of the total mission-advancement process. This is the primary role of a director of development: to work closely with the bishop, pastor, religious superior or chief administrator, and with other members of the organization's leadership team, *to manage the process of planning, communications and resource development so that the Church's mission can be carried out as successfully as possible.*

The consistent experience of organizations and institutions that have successful fundraising programs underscores the importance of a team approach to mission advancement that can be summarized briefly as follows:
*   First, articulate your vision and plans.
*   Then, build ownership and support for this shared vision and priorities.
*   Finally, develop the human, physical and financial resources you need to realize your vision.

6. Why does mission advancement begin with a statement of vision? How does a vision statement help carry out the work of the Church in a particular diocese, parish, religious community or other Catholic organization?

Bishops and other Church leaders sometimes shy away from the request that they articulate a vision—particularly when they are first assigned to a diocese or a new leadership position. But the desire to hear, and affirm, the leader's vision for the future is widespread among Catholics who look to their leaders for spiritual and moral guidance—and, above all, for a genuine sense of hope—especially in times of crisis or uncertainty. Mission advancement takes full advantage of this desire for leadership and vision by providing the bishop, pastor, religious superior or chief administrator with consultative processes for developing and communicating a clear sense of vision for the future.

In a Catholic organization, a vision statement must always be built on the received mission of the Church as it has been given to us in Sacred Scripture and in the teachings of the Magisterium. At the same time, a vision statement can provide opportunities for religious leaders to emphasize the unique circumstances (challenges and opportunities) facing the Church in a particular time and place. Most importantly, a vision statement can help the bishop, religious superior or chief administrator articulate pastoral priorities and invite members of the clergy, religious and faithful to help carry out Christ's missionary work at home and beyond diocesan or institutional boundaries.

A vision statement does not have to be lengthy. As clearly and simply as possible, it should provide answers to the following questions:

1. Who are we and who are we called to become as disciples of Jesus Christ and members of this particular community of faith?

2. What is the mission of the Church always and everywhere? How does this mission speak to us—concretely—in this time and in this place?

3. What are the unique gifts and strengths of this diocese, religious community or Catholic organization? What is the legacy entrusted to us by those who have gone before us in faith? How are we called to preserve and pass on this legacy of faith, hope and love?

4. What are the distinctive opportunities and challenges presented to us now as we seek to carry out the Church's mission here in this time and in this place?

5. What are our priorities—for the spiritual growth of our people? For lifelong faith formation? For the ministry of charity? For justice and peace? For evangelization? For vocations? For addressing other urgent needs or taking advantage of special opportunities?

6. What strategies or action plans can we develop in order to most effectively respond to these opportunities and challenges? What programs or activities can provide specific, measurable responses to our most urgent needs and priorities?

7. What resources (human and financial) do we need to carry out the work of Christ here and now?

8. How will we hold ourselves accountable for the implementation of these pastoral plans and priorities? How will we measure our success—especially in areas like spiritual growth or liturgical and sacramental celebrations that do not easily lend themselves to quantitative measurement?

Obviously, a bishop, pastor, religious superior or chief administrator should not attempt to answer all these questions by himself or herself. Instead, the leader should engage members of his or her leadership team, consultative bodies, priests, deacons and religious, and as many lay leaders as is practical in the circumstances of the diocese, parish, religious community, school or other Catholic organization.

The first four questions above call for prayerful reflection and discussion of the mission of the Church and the leader's vision. The final four require pastoral planning activities that can help translate the leader's vision into specific action steps and systems of accountability.

Much more needs to be said about the kinds of processes that are appropriate and effective for developing and implementing a vision statement and pastoral plan in a Catholic organization. To the extent possible, such processes should be simple, focused and as specific as possible. This desire for simplicity and manageability often conflicts with the equally important desire to engage as many people as possible in the process. This is one of the most significant challenges in mission advancement—to accomplish broad involvement and ownership of a vision and plan that are as simple and achievable as possible!

Clearly, success will require patience. Perhaps this is why the Fathers of Vatican Council II reminded us that the Church's mission will not be accomplished quickly: *"While she slowly grows to maturity, the Church longs for the completed kingdom and, with all her strength, hopes and desires to be united in glory with her king"* (*Lumen Gentium,* the Dogmatic Constitution on the Church, #5).

7.   Why is planning essential to mission advancement?

Successful fundraising requires a "case" or at least a cause that is worthy of financial support. Relief for hurricane victims is a worthy cause. So is tuition assistance for families who otherwise could not afford to send their children to Catholic schools. But the comprehensive, long-term process we call mission advancement requires more than just a good cause or a well-developed case for support—as important as these are for the purposes of professional fundraising. For one thing, a Catholic organization's case may include many worthwhile causes. Which is more important—Disaster relief? Tuition assistance? Evangelization? Funding for vocations programs? Building new parishes? Capital improvements at the seminary? Consolidating or closing parishes?

The list could go on and on. Yes, Catholic organizations need a compelling case for financial support, but in order to formulate this case, a plan and a clear statement of priorities must be developed.

Mission advancement requires a plan to help build confidence among those who will be asked to help carry out the mission of the organization in the face of many obstacles and uncertainties. Catholics have shown that they can deal with confusion, anxiety and even scandal, but it helps if they know that their leaders have a clear, focused and achievable plan for carry out the work of the Church.

The plan does not have to be elaborate (or expensive). It shouldn't take years to develop or decades to implement. The plan should be an outgrowth of the Church's mission. It should be designed to adapt the timeless program and plan of the Gospel to the concrete needs of the community here and now. It helps if the plan is simple and action-oriented. It is also a good idea to involve as many clergy, religious and lay people as possible in the early stages of the planning process so that the plan will have broad ownership and support when it is ready to be promulgated and implemented.

Catholic organizations do planning in a number of different ways—from formal processes that involve thousands of people in many different geographic regions to simpler, more tightly focused processes involving just a representative group of council members or other planners appointed by the bishop, pastor, religious superior or chief administrator. Some bishops convoke a diocesan synod, which is a formal, juridical process. Others work quietly behind the scenes to develop their plans in consultation with representatives of the people being served.

Whatever planning method the organization uses, some common elements are important to the overall mission-advancement process. These include:

1. A discovery or discernment phase that involves a representative cross section of the Catholic community in identifying and reflecting on the strengths, weaknesses, opportunities and threats that the organization faces as it attempts to carry out the Church's mission in this time and in this place.

2. A plan-development process that can establish major long-term goals and priorities for bringing the vision to fulfillment. This process should be consultative, but it should not be bogged down by efforts to achieve the full support of everyone. Consensus-building is a desired outcome, but it is not always possible—especially among groups with strongly held interests or concerns.

3. Specific action plans (containing measurable benchmarks, timelines, accountability and costs or sources of funding) for

each priority. These are the concrete programs and activities that will make sure diocesan goals and priorities actually get put into practice and are more than just wishful thinking.

4. A system for reviewing, adjusting and, when necessary, re-working action steps on a regular basis in order to make sure the plan does not "sit on a shelf" but remains a living document that is responsive to the changing needs of the Church and society.

Any planning process that can accomplish the four steps noted above will be an invaluable tool for building confidence among clergy and laity and for managing the day-to-day operations of the organization on a proactive basis. The work of mission advancement is greatly assisted when the organization's leadership team has a vision statement and plan that is understood, accepted and supported by members of the Catholic community and by the individuals, families and organizations that can help develop the resources that are needed to carry out the mission and plans of a diocese, parish, religious community, school or other Catholic organization.

8. What role do communications play in a successful mission-advancement program?

Everything! Today, perhaps more than ever, advancing the mission of the Church requires excellent communications. The Church's mission is to proclaim the Kingdom of God and to be the seed and beginning of that Kingdom. It is the Word of God that we proclaim, and it is Christ's work that we carry on as disciples and stewards of all God's gifts. Mission advancement in the Catholic Church is inconceivable without communications. And all the instruments of communications that are available to Christians in the 21st century must be employed—as completely and professionally as possible—in the proclamation of the Kingdom and the advancement of Christ's work on earth.

St. Paul was the Church's first great communicator. He intuitively knew the value of using the means of communication available to him to keep the faith communities he founded engaged, focused, challenged and inspired. In fact, all of the New Testament is an inspired outreach, a series of communications between the earliest evangelists and the growing but dispersed People of God. (St. Paul was also the Church's first great fundraiser—using all his influence to urge the communities he served to give generously on behalf of priorities that extended far beyond the local needs of individual churches.)

Mission advancement requires excellent, effective communications. Unless we can capture people's attention, they will be distracted by all the other messages they receive daily through the news and entertainment media, advertising, the Internet and much more. The days are long past when a letter from the bishop read during Sunday Mass or published in the diocesan newspaper or parish bulletin is all that's needed. Today, a Church leader who wants to be heard must take advantage of many diverse instruments of communication. Leaders must be seen and heard at every possible opportunity, and the message must be clear and compelling. The alternative is to be overlooked or to be drowned out by the constant, unrelenting flow of messages that are communicated to individuals and families at nearly every moment of every day.

In the Church, mission advancement is closely related to evangelization. We do not proclaim the Gospel in order to develop human and financial resources. That would be placing the cart before the horse. But resources are needed *in order to evangelize* and, what's more, the instruments of communication used to evangelize are the very same media that are necessary to capture people's attention, to engage them in the sacramental life of the Church and in its ministry and to invite people to share their gifts of time, talent and treasure in order to carry out Christ's work.

Mission advancement requires organizations that are serious about generating much-needed human and financial resources to develop a case for support. This is a traditional fundraising tool that is designed to articulate compelling reasons why a particular organization deserves the sacrificial gifts of individuals and groups who share the organization's values and who want to be involved in realizing its vision and goals. The essential elements of a "compelling case" are that it should:

- Capture people's attention
- Provide important information
- Stimulate personal engagement in the organization's mission and priorities
- Inspire people to give generously.

Without question, the most effective way to communicate the case for support is through personal witness. Brochures, DVDs, Web sites, e-newsletters, newspaper articles and advertisements are important instruments of communication, but they are means to an end, not the end itself, which should always be *personal* communication. Various media can be used to supplement and reinforce communication of the organization's vision, plan and priority needs. But they can *never* take the place of face-to-face communication between the bishop, pastor, religious superior or chief administrator and people who have the capacity to help advance the organization's mission.

With this in mind, individual and small-group meetings are the best way to "make the case" for a diocese, parish, religious community, school or other Catholic organization. Special events, printed and audiovisual communications, e-mail and Web sites, newspapers and printed materials are important, but secondary, means of reinforcing messages that are most effective when they are delivered as personally as possible.

Every successful mission-advancement program should have a comprehensive communications plan. This plan, which presumes that the organization has already articulated its vision, mission and priorities, should address the following questions:

1. What's the most effective way to express our vision and priorities? Our Case for Support?

2. Who are the individuals and groups that we need to inform, involve, inspire and invite as we communicate our case?

3. How many individual (face-to-face) meetings can we schedule?

4. What kinds of small-group activities and special events should we include in our communications plan?

5. What kind of print, audiovisual and electronic communications can we employ?

6. What are our strategies for media relations—both positively and in times of crisis?

A comprehensive communications plan that takes advantage of all the means of communication available to a diocese, parish, religious community, school or other Catholic organization is a *sine qua non* for mission advancement. Especially today, our communications must be more than satisfactory. They must be exemplary. Proclamation of God's Kingdom, which is the mission of the Church, deserves no less than excellent communications.

Questions for reflection and discussion

1. What is mission advancement? How is it related to discipleship and evangelization?

2. What is the mission of the Church? How does "advancement" contribute to carrying out this mission?

3. How is mission advancement different in a Catholic diocese?

4. What is the role of the bishop in mission advancement?

5. Successful mission advancement requires a team. Why?

6. Why does mission advancement begin with a statement of vision? How does a vision statement help carry out the work of the Church in a particular diocese, parish, religious community or other Catholic organization.

7. Why is planning essential to mission advancement?

8. What role do communications play in a successful mission-advancement program?

❧ Prayer ❧

Lord Jesus Christ, before you ascended into heaven you gave us the great commission to "Go out into the whole world and baptize in the name of the Father, Son and Holy Spirit."

Help us be faithful stewards of this mission. We believe that you have given us everything we need to proclaim the coming Kingdom of God and to be the seeds and beginning of that Kingdom here and now.

May the Holy Spirit sustain us in this great work. And may we look forward in hope to the day when God's reign is established once and for all throughout all creation. Amen

Best practices in professional fundraising

Provided that the basic approach is consistent with the theology and practice of stewardship, the principles and techniques of professional fundraising can be extremely helpful to the overall stewardship and development efforts of the parish or diocese (U.S. BISHOPS, "STEWARDSHIP AND DEVELOPMENT IN CATHOLIC DIOCESES AND PARISHES: A RESOURCE MANUAL," P.61).

1. What is the relationship between the spirituality of stewardship and the best practices of professional fundraising?

Unfortunately, we have so often confused stewardship with fundraising that people have come to associate these terms as being completely interchangeable. Stewardship is not fundraising. And it's a grave mistake to confuse these two very different concepts. But does that mean they have nothing to do with each other? Or that we dare not utter these two terms—*stewardship* and *fundraising*—in the same breath?

Stewardship is a way of life, a practical form of spirituality, a disciple's response in faith to the Lord's invitation to be his disciple. Stewardship requires conversion. It requires letting go of selfishness and sin; giving up our preoccupation with material things, with status and prestige. It means following Jesus without counting the cost and carrying forward his work in the world.

Disciples of Jesus Christ are given a mission—the great commission—to go out to the whole world and proclaim the good news; to feed the poor, heal the sick and comfort those in sorrow or distress. Stewardship is discipleship in action, a form of spirituality for daily Christian living. It's about much, much more than money. It's about everything we do in our daily lives—how we cultivate and develop all God's gifts (spiritual and material)—and it's about sharing generously with others our time, our skills and abilities and, yes, our money (which is also a gift from God that we are called to share).

So stewardship is much more than fundraising, and the two terms should never be confused or used interchangeably, but isn't there an important—essential—connection between teaching stewardship as a way of life and advancing the Church's mission? If there were no connection between stewardship and mission advancement, there would be no connection between discipleship and Christian service or between spirituality and the ministry of charity. If there were no connection between stewardship education and professional, ethical fundraising, there would be no link between our motivation for giving (gratitude to God and a profound sense of responsibility to give and share with others) and the occasions for giving that are presented to us in the Sunday collection or our school's annual appeal or the diocese's annual appeal.

There *must* be a connection between the spirituality of stewardship and our efforts to advance the mission of the Church. Otherwise our fundraising activities are reduced to ends in themselves, tails that wag the dog, necessary evils that require pure and pristine spiritual people to dirty their hands with the filthy lucre of money and fundraising.

That is not the vision of the U.S. bishops' pastoral letter *Stewardship: A Disciple's Response;* it is not a Catholic view of the relationship between spirit and matter or between faith and daily living. Stewardship views all of

God's creation as good and all of it as gift. There is nothing unclean or evil about fundraising—provided that it is motivated by genuine principles of stewardship and philanthropy. And there is nothing demeaning about fundraising activity (whether direct or indirect) provided that it is ethical, disciplined and reflective of the best practices of development and institutional advancement.

2.   How do we identify and implement best practices?

The U.S. bishops' pastoral letter *Stewardship: A Disciple's Response* admonishes Catholic organizations that the practice of good stewardship requires that dioceses, parishes, religious communities, schools and other Catholic organizations "observe the most stringent ethical, legal and fiscal standards." In addition, the tenth anniversary edition of the pastoral letter on stewardship contains an appendix entitled "Stewardship and Development in Catholic Dioceses and Parishes: A Resource Manual" that clearly states the bishops' position on the use of fundraising practices. According to this resource manual, "Within a total stewardship context, parishes and dioceses should not hesitate to use the best available ethically sound fundraising practices to ask Catholic people to make financial contributions that are planned, proportionate, and sacrificial. Provided that the basic approach is consistent with the theology and practice of stewardship, the principles and techniques of professional fundraising can be extremely helpful to the overall stewardship and development efforts of the parish or diocese" (p. 61).

In order to be good stewards of the mission entrusted to us by Christ as his disciples, we must use the very best tools or instruments available to us. Without question, this includes the best practices of professional fundraising.

Dan Schipp, who served as vice president for development at Saint Meinrad Archabbey and School of Theology for more than 20 years, has suggested the following as best practices for successful fundraising:

1.   **Communications.** Be intentional about your messages. Be careful to communicate your vision and priorities in ways that engage people who share your values. Tell stories that illustrate your message and that can inspire others. Appoint an small group of people who have no vested interest and will be objective to review all your communications and evaluate their effectiveness.

2.   **Annual giving.** Make sure that your annual appeal is more than just a sophisticated second collection. Use it as an opportunity to engage people of faith in your mission and priorities. The primary goal of your annual giving efforts should be to increase participa-

tion in the mission of the Church. This means much more than just increasing the number of donors (as important as that is) or the amount raised (as necessary as that is). Increasing participation means growing the number of people who are personally engaged in the ministries supported by their fundraising dollars—through their prayer, their active interest, and, where possible, through their gifts of time and talent as well as treasure. To succeed at increasing participation at this much more profound level, your annual giving programs will need to be creative, inspirational and truly engaging.

3. **Major gifts.** Be attentive to the 10 percent who give 90 percent of your organization's philanthropic dollars. This does not mean you should ignore, or fail to appreciate, the many small gifts you receive (the widow's mite). It does mean that you must be proactive and systematic in your efforts to invite, and challenge, people who have the capacity to make significant gifts to help advance the Church's mission. Many Church leaders are uncomfortable asking for major gifts. That's OK. The primary role of the bishop, pastor, religious superior or chief administrator is to articulate vision and to speak about the impact that a leadership gift can have on the Church's ability to carry out Christ's work. Someone else, a volunteer leader or advancement staff member, can "ask for the gift." What's important is that the organization has a professional major-gifts program that is constantly identifying and evaluating prospects, building strong relationships with potential lead donors and finding appropriate ways to invite people of means to make substantial investments in the Church's mission. Catholic universities and other institutions, like Saint Meinrad, have been doing this very successfully for many years, but even at these organizations major gifts don't just happen. They are the result of much hard work and the commitment of significant time and resources by the organization's leaders.

4. **Chart your progress.** Mission advancement is a systematic process. It is important to develop benchmarks and strategic indicators to help gauge whether or not you are accomplishing your objectives (which should include the number of donors, amounts raised and levels of active participation). Pay attention to what your strategic indicators are telling you. Make adjustments as necessary and never be satisfied with the status quo. When times are tough economically, strive to increase the number of small gifts and encourage major donors to make sacrificial gifts to help make

up for those who can no longer afford to give as much as they did when times were good. Most important of all, grow your relationships! People who believe in your efforts to carry out the mission of the Church will remain faithful to that mission in good times and in bad.

5. **Engage everyone.** Members of your stewardship and development staff should consider themselves partners to the bishop, pastor, religious superior or chief administrators in the work of mission advancement. No one should be simply collecting a pay check. Take seriously the spirituality of stewardship and encourage your staff and volunteers to grow spiritually, to see themselves as ministers of hospitality who invite others to share in the vision and priorities of your organization. If your volunteer leaders and staff members are inspired and engaged, they will be much more effective at inspiring and engaging others.

No conflict exists between stewardship and the best practices of professional fundraising—as long as the tail doesn't wag the dog. On the contrary, fundraising practices that complement and encourage stewardship principles of gratitude, responsibility, generosity and the willingness to give back to God with increase are strongly recommended to all who are responsible for advancing the Church's mission.

3. Giving to religion is closely tied to participation.

What does weekly Mass attendance have to do with weekly giving? Would Catholics' financial support of their parish or diocese increase if they were more involved in the Church's prayer and work?

Independent research into giving to religious organizations of diverse Jewish, Christian and Islamic faiths suggests that *active involvement* is the single most important factor in giving to faith-based causes or organizations. This represents a significant challenge at a time when research conducted by Indiana University's Center on Philanthropy Panel Study (COPPS) shows that "religious giving and attendance at weekly services have declined in general across the nation, and younger generations attend services less frequently."

According to Bill Enright, who directs the Center on Philanthropy's Lake Institute on Faith and Giving, the decline in attendance at places of worship can be attributed to what researchers call "the loss of the Sabbath." Because fewer people today set aside a sacred day for worship, presence and participation have declined and, proportionately, so has financial support. COPPS researchers compared two different generations of donors' giving patterns over a 40-year period. The results are conclusive. It doesn't matter which religious tradition is represented. The more often people attend their synagogue, church or mosque and participate in its mission, the more generous they are in their financial support.

These independent research findings, which are reported in the Center on Philanthropy's *Philanthropy Matters* (Volume 16, Issue 1, 2008), underscore the close relationship that exists between evangelization and stewardship (or between active engagement in the life of the Church and the willingness to share generously with others). To the extent that Catholics (and people of all faiths) are present and active, they give themselves—time, talent and treasure—to support the Church's mission. It's as simple (and as complex) as that.

We do not preach the Gospel (evangelization) or teach of the joy of giving (stewardship) in order to increase financial support. But we also cannot ignore the fact that *active engagement* is critical to mission advancement. If we want to grow the resources that are needed to carry out the Church's mission, we must find new ways to involve Catholics of all ages and from diverse economic, social and cultural backgrounds in the worship and the ministry of their Church.

4. Where are the Church's million-dollar donors?

A strange paradox in charitable giving in the United States is rarely discussed.

The largest total amount of charitable dollars contributed by Americans (nearly $100 billion each year or one-third of all donations) goes to support religious causes. But when it comes to individual gifts of $1 million or more, churches and other faith-based organizations are near the bottom of the list (just 2 percent).

Why do our nation's largest donors shy away from making sizeable contributions to the Church? What does this fact say about giving to religion— or about the fundraising and financial management practices of faith-based organizations?

It may be helpful to look at the organizations who do receive multimillion-dollar gifts. How are they different from religious organizations? What motivates wealthy donors to make big gifts to these institutions? What do churches and other faith-based organizations have to learn from them?

According to an article in *The Chronicle of Philanthropy*, January 10, 2008, by far the lion's share of multimillion-dollar gifts goes to higher education. Based on a study by the Institute for Jewish and Community Research, conducted between 2001 and 2003, 25 percent of all gifts of $1 million or more went to private higher education. Another 19 percent went to public higher education—making colleges and universities the single largest beneficiary of multimillion-dollar gifts (44 percent). Next come gifts to health and medicine (16 percent) and arts and culture (12 percent). Following these are gifts to human services, other educational institutions and purposes, the environment and international causes that range from 5 percent to 3 percent of the total. Religion and other charities are at the bottom, ranging from 2 percent to 1 percent of the total.

Why would higher education, health care and the arts get significantly more large gifts than churches or other faith-based organizations? No studies or objective research projects have been done on this question, so any response will have to be based on intuition and observation rather than empirical evidence. With this caveat in mind, the following can be suggested as possible reasons why wealthy individuals and foundations don't make as many million-dollar gifts to religion as they do to other nonprofit organizations—especially higher education, health care and the arts.

1. Frequently today, leaders in higher education, health care and the arts are chosen because of their ability to attract (and solicit) large gifts. Regardless of their other skills, talents and credentials, today's leaders of the most successful fundraising organizations are required to have a proven track record at raising mega gifts. This is rarely true for the leaders of religious organizations who are almost always chosen for pastoral reasons and who frequently resist the financial management and fundraising dimensions of religious leadership.

2. Giving to higher education, health care and the arts is prestigious in ways that giving to religion is not. This begs the question why this is so, but it can be argued that naming a science building, a hospital or a center for the performing arts means more to wealthy donors than being recognized as the largest donor to a church or a center for ministry. What does this say about our social or cultural values? What can be done to make faith-based giving more "prestigious"—assuming this is appropriate or desirable?

3. Compare the size and expertise of finance offices and fundraising staffs of any faith-based organization in the United States to its counterpart in higher education, health care or the arts. The differences are astounding. The most successful fundraising organizations have learned over the years that to raise large amounts of money from individuals and philanthropic organizations you must demonstrate your credibility as a fiscally sound organization, and you have to build-up your capacity for fundraising (especially in the area of major gifts).

Is it possible to help wealthy donors recognize the importance of making big gifts to religious organizations? Many religious leaders fear that the changes they would have to make in order to attract multimillion-dollar gifts would dilute their identity as faith-based organizations. These concerns should not be minimized. At the same time, it's fair to ask whether the mission and goals of religious organizations aren't every bit as worthy of significant philanthropic support as those of higher education, health care and the arts. Surely we can find ways to help faith-based organizations do a better job of making the case for the larger "transformational" gifts.

This is a subject that requires careful research, discussion and planning.

5. What makes a capital campaign successful?

A capital campaign is an extraordinary fundraising program. Most of the time it is extraordinary in two ways: First, the project for which funds are being raised is above and beyond the daily activities of the organization (a new building or renovation, debt reduction, endowment, etc.). Second, a capital campaign is extraordinary because it normally asks donors to make substantial commitments over and above their ordinary giving and to stretch these out over a multiyear pledge period.

There are three things you have to do in order to have a successful capital campaign.

First, you have to develop and communicate a compelling case. That means you have to identify a genuine need, and you have to help people become personally committed to making a difference in the world by helping meet that need through this capital campaign.

The second thing you have to do in a capital campaign is to motivate and involve a large number of volunteers. You can't conduct an extraordinary fundraising program by direct mail or by taking up a second collection. Successful capital campaigns are the result of strong, committed leadership (for example, from the bishop, the pastor, and key lay leaders). But leadership from the top down is not enough. Successful campaigns also require the active, grassroots involvement of women and men in many different facets of the organization—each performing important but manageable tasks within the overall campaign structure. This requires a great deal of organization and discipline, which is why military images (campaign, strategy, etc.) have historically been used to describe the fundamental tasks associated with this extraordinary form of fundraising.

The third thing you have to do in a capital campaign is to ask people to make substantial financial commitments at levels of giving that stretch their ability to give. This is the part of the campaign that most everybody hates—the moment when someone (the organization's leader or a volunteer) has to ask someone else to make what is for them a substantial commitment—a sacrificial gift that is proportionate to their means.

As most of us know from experience, there is no easy way around this fundamental requirement. Someone has to ask for the gift. You can soft-pedal the ask by burying it in a letter or by doing it in a generalized way at a large gathering of people. When all is said and done, the only really effective way to solicit substantial gifts (of whatever size) is by a personal, individual, face-to-face invitation.

That's the bad news about capital campaigns: someone has to ask for the gift. The good news is that with a compelling case, strong leadership and active volunteers, and the right kind of personal invitation, millions of people each year throughout the United States make substantial commitments of their time, talent and money to meet the extraordinary needs presented to them in capital campaigns.

But what about the distinctive religious mission of dioceses, parishes, religious communities, schools and other Catholic organizations? Can a capital campaign be financially successful and still be faithful to the Church's mission? Can a successful capital campaign also be an occasion for teaching principles of Christian stewardship?

Yes! A capital campaign can be an excellent opportunity to teach principles of Christian stewardship and to challenge people of faith to make substantial commitments of time, talent and treasure based on prayerful discernment of God's will.

Why do we believe this? Because we have seen it happen many times in many different places and circumstances. With our own eyes, we have witnessed many minor miracles, experiences of *metanoia,* or conversion, that have signified an extraordinary spiritual change in the lives of ordinary people.

A capital campaign that is based on stewardship principles has to do what any successful capital fundraising program does. It has to develop and communicate a compelling case, it has to have strong leadership and many active volunteers; and it has to issue a personal invitation to make an extraordinary, substantial commitment. That's the standard operating procedure for any capital campaign—at an art museum, the state university, or a Catholic parish. A stewardship-based campaign preserves the best aspects of professional capital fundraising and adds something more. It begins, or reinforces, a process of stewardship education and formation that must continue long after the capital campaign is over, and it invites people to discern God's will in their lives, which is always a much more challenging personal invitation than simply asking for a one-time financial commitment.

By teaching principles of Christian stewardship, by emphasizing prayer and discernment, and by providing Catholics with concrete opportunities to participate in the mission and ministries of their diocese, parish, religious community, school or another Catholic institution, an integrated approach to stewardship and capital fundraising can make a real difference—in the lives of families, the school, the religious community, the parish and the diocese. It can raise the money needed to fund Church ministries while, at the same, provide opportunities for genuine spiritual growth.

Yes, a capital campaign can make a difference—by raising urgently needed capital resources, by involving many different people in the Church's mission and by serving as an occasion for spiritual growth.

6. What about planned giving?

Efforts to provide individuals and families with information about planned giving should be integrated into the diocese's or parish's overall stewardship education program. If properly presented as a means of exercising responsible stewardship of their accumulated assets and as an opportunity to make a distinctive contribution to the mission and ministries of the Church, an educational program designed to promote planned giving can be a double service to Church members. It can remind them of their overall stewardship responsibility and, at the same time, provide very practical suggestions on how to increase income, save taxes, and contribute to the Church ("Stewardship and Development in Catholic Dioceses and Parishes: A Resource Manual," p. 58).

Planned giving provides Catholic organizations with unique opportunities to teach stewardship principles and, at the same time, develop substantial resources to carry forward the Church's mission. A planned, or deferred, gift is ordinarily a contribution that is made from assets rather than from income. As a result, it requires careful planning to minimize costs and maximize benefits to both the donor and the organization that is designated as the recipient of the gift. The most common form of planned gift is a bequest in someone's Last Will and Testament. Other forms of planned gifts include charitable gift annuities, gifts of real estate or insurance, and charitable remainder trusts. The connection between stewardship and planned giving is straightforward: a planned gift represents the donor's stewardship of his or her estate beyond death. It is an act that signifies "taking care of and sharing" (one of the definitions of stewardship) the donor's accumulated assets, his or her life estate.

Most Catholic organizations have some experience with the benefits of an unexpected bequest. An increasing number of dioceses, parishes, religious communities, schools and other Catholic organizations encourage planned giving in their promotional materials, on their Web sites and even in annual appeals and capital campaigns. Here are just a few "helpful hints" for encouraging planned gifts:

1. Keep it simple. In the beginning, focus on wills. As time goes on, more sophisticated planned-giving instruments can be offered.

2. Focus on key prospects. Every member of the Catholic community should know about general planned-giving opportunities, but only a relatively small segment of the community is ready, or interested, now. Age, family situation, accumulated assets, prior giving history and level of commitment to the organization and its mission are all factors that need to be taken into consideration when "marketing" planned gifts.

3. Include information about bequests, and perhaps other forms of planned giving, in all printed materials and mailings. Consider including brief reminders in annual appeal literature and pledge reminders—as well as in bulletins, newsletters and other forms of communication.

4. Sponsor "Will Seminars" or other gatherings that provide helpful information about estate planning in general and planned-gift opportunities in particular. These should be low-key, educational offerings—not sales pitches. The participation of attorneys, estate planners and other professional advisors can be extremely beneficial—provided their objective is to educate not to sell.

5. Personalized mailings that include information about planned gifts or that invite recipients to attend seminars can be a very effective way to introduce members of the Catholic community to planned-giving opportunities. However, follow-up is important—through phone calls, personal visits or invitations to attend events sponsored by the organization.

6. Finally, an increasing number of Catholic organizations have established "recognition" or "legacy" societies for individuals who have made some form of bequest to the Church. Although membership in these societies comes after a planned gift has been disclosed, experience suggests that the increased contact and involvement of society members often results in additional or increased gifts.

Although planned gifts frequently have favorable tax benefits associated with them, the vast majority of planned gift donors are primarily motivated by the opportunity to participate in the mission of the Church in a substantial way. Here again, stewardship principles of gratitude, responsibility, generosity and the willingness to give back to the Lord with increase are closely connected to planned giving as a way of taking care of, and sharing, blessings received during the donor's lifetime.

7. Is the work of mission advancement a ministry, a profession, or both?

What is a director of development? Is she or he a fundraising professional or a minister of stewardship? If the answer is "a little of both," how do we distinguish what is ministerial from what is professional? Can we really have it both ways, or does one aspect of the work suffer because of the demands made by the other?

Professional fundraisers sometimes criticize the Church because of a perceived reluctance to be aggressive—especially in the area of major-gifts development. Ministry personnel worry that practices of finance and fundraising will overshadow more fundamental pastoral concerns. Where do we find the right balance between ministry and administration or between the Church's spiritual and temporal affairs? Can the work of mission advancement effectively integrate these distinct, but equally necessary, spheres of the Church's daily life?

Mission advancement requires a profound integration of the Church's spiritual and temporal affairs. The Church's mission is spiritual and sacramental—to proclaim the Kingdom of God and to be the seed and beginning of that Kingdom. But the realization of that mission, including evangelization, worship and sacramental ministry, faith formation, charity and justice, is also temporal and institutional. To advance the mission of the Church, we must minister to God's people. But we must also attend to the administrative affairs of Church life, which, especially in complex societies, have become increasingly professional.

A director of stewardship and development in a Catholic organization must be a professional person who has a keen sense of ministry. He or she must have a genuine "heart" for the mission and ministries of the Church and, at the same time, possess the skills and experience necessary to manage the overall advancement process.

As a professional, a development director is responsible for *managing the processes* that are required for effective mission advancement. This includes three essential functions of 1) leadership and planning, 2) communications and relationship building, and 3) inviting participation and financial support. The director cannot (and should not) try to do all these things by herself or himself. Successful mission advancement requires a team that includes executive leadership, volunteer advocates and professional staff. But someone has to manage the various processes to make sure that they happen and are coordinated with one another. This is a professional responsibility that requires skill and experience.

As a minister, the development director is responsible for *seeing that principles of Christian stewardship are fully integrated into the advancement program* and that the invitation to participate in the organization's work is based on a genuine understanding of and appreciation for the Church's mission. The ministry of fundraising recognizes that genuine spiritual growth is possible when people accept the Lord's invitation to give generously of themselves (their time, talent and treasure) out of gratitude to God and with a profound sense of responsibility for the welfare of others.

In a Catholic diocese, for example, the director of mission advancement participates in the bishop's ministry to teach, sanctify and provide pastoral leadership for the local Church. This requires a genuine integration of the spiritual and temporal—first of all on the part of the bishop but also on the part of those who assist him in his pastoral responsibilities.

So, we can say that the director of stewardship helps the bishop *teach* by:
- Encouraging him to articulate vision and priorities
- Assisting in the development of the diocese's case for support
- Offering "talking points" when the bishop meets with donors or speaks at diocesan events
- Drafting letters to donors—both before and after they have supported the work of the diocese.

Similarly, the development director helps the bishop *sanctify* by:
- Promoting the spirituality of stewardship
- Making prayer an integral part of all fundraising activities
- Inviting members of the Catholic community to make gifts of time, talent and treasure that are prayerful, planned, proportionate and sacrificial.

Finally, a director of mission advancement helps the bishop *provide pastoral leadership* by:
- Engaging clergy and lay leaders in all stewardship and development activities
- Designing and managing professional advancement programs—using "the most stringent legal, ethical and fiscal standards" and the best practices of stewardship education and professional fundraising
- Building up the local Church through growing its human and financial resources.

In a very real way, the director of development in a diocese is a steward (understood as guardian, caretaker or manager) of the bishop's responsibility to advance the mission of the Church. He or she carries out this stewardship responsibility by helping the diocese model good stewardship by:

- Saying thank you
- Being accountable
- Sharing gifts generously—out of justice and charity
- Growing, and giving back, all God's spiritual and material gifts.

Whether the organization is a diocese, parish, religious community, school or other Catholic organization, the work of mission advancement must combine both the effectiveness of the Church's ministry and the successful management of the organization's temporal affairs. Mission advancement is not a necessary evil. It's a means to an end—the successful carrying forward of Christ's work on earth. And the work of the development director in any Catholic organization is a profession, and a ministry, both of which must be wholly dedicated to advancing the Church's mission.

Questions for reflection and discussion

1. What is the relationship between the spirituality of stewardship and the best practices of professional fundraising?

2. How do we identify and implement best practices?

3. Why is giving to religion closely tied to participation?

4. Where are the Church's million-dollar donors?

5. What makes a capital campaign successful?

6. How does planned giving help individuals and organizations practice stewardship of all God's gifts ?

7. Is the work of mission advancement a ministry, a profession, or both?

❧ Prayer ❧

Loving Father, you alone are the source of every good gift. We praise you for all your gifts to us, and we thank you for your abundant generosity.

Everything we have, and all that we are, comes from you. Help us be grateful and responsible.

We commit ourselves to being good stewards. Help us develop and share your gifts with others as you have generously shared yourself with us.

We make this prayer through Jesus Christ our Lord, who lives and reigns with you and the Holy Spirit, now and forever. Amen.

Lessons from the road: My mission-advancement story

Everything I know about mission advancement I learned from others. As a young development officer, I was uniquely blessed to have a series of mentors who guided my professional growth and helped me make important connections between my personal understanding and practice of the Catholic faith and my experiences as a professional in the field of mission advancement. The following is my "mission-advancement story." In it, I acknowledge some remarkably gifted people who served with distinction in this frequently misunderstood area of the Church's ministry and who were very gracious and generous to me in the years that I worked with them. I have tried to practice what I learned from them, my mentors in the field of mission advancement, and to reflect on it and share it with others as they did.

1. Development at Saint Meinrad Archabbey and Seminary

My association with "development" goes back more than 40 years. In 1967, I was a freshman at a seminary college operated by the Benedictine monks of Saint Meinrad Archabbey. During my freshman orientation that year, a distinguished, white-haired gentleman named John S. MacCauley gave a talk on "development." John was Saint Meinrad's first professional development officer, and this was one of his first efforts to outline his vision of what development could mean for a religious institution like Saint Meinrad. I remember very little about that talk. (As a college freshman, there were many other things on my mind!) But in the next dozen years, I heard John talk about development many times in many different settings and circumstances. And I came to believe in John MacCauley's vision of development—and to stake my professional life on the possibility of sharing this vision with others—especially with bishops and other Church leaders.

I spent eight years at Saint Meinrad as a student (four years in college and four years in the graduate School of Theology). During many of these years, I worked in the development office, and I came to regard John Mac-Cauley as a friend and mentor. He was kind enough to invite me to his home, make me part of his family, and share with me his deep and abiding faith. As is often true of young people, I took those years for granted.

In 1975, I left the seminary and became a religion teacher at a Jesuit high school in my hometown of Cleveland. During this time, I met my future wife, Sharon, at a high school basketball game. (Her younger brothers were my students.) And a year later, we were married. When our first child was on her way, and the prospect of mortgage payments and all that goes with that set in, I quickly came to the conclusion that I was not meant to teach high school for the rest of my life. So, after four years of teaching, I started looking around. One of my uncles offered me the chance to join his insurance agency, but that was not for me. A friend's father, who owned a trucking supply company, wanted me to come to work for him, but that didn't seem right either.

Then one day, John MacCauley called. Saint Meinrad had received a grant from Lilly Endowment Inc. to hire and train a planned-giving officer. John asked if I was interested. I was so excited I could hardly contain myself. But it's safe to say that my bride of six months, who was expecting our first child, was less than thrilled. I was asking Sharon to leave a large, loving family in Cleveland and to settle in rural southern Indiana, so that I could become a development officer. It was the first of many sacrificial gifts that my wife and family have made over the years so that I could pursue my unique vocation.

Not long after I joined the staff at Saint Meinrad, I was invited to become part of the initial group of seminary development officers who formed the Development and Institutional Advancement Program for the Association of Theological Schools in the U.S. and Canada (ATS), and that experience was invaluable. Working closely with many skilled, professional, faith-filled women and men was a real inspiration. I know that there are good people in every profession, but something about seminary development officers really appealed to me. Looking back, I think it was the combination of personal faith and professional skills that attracted me. But whatever it was, I know that I wanted to be what they were: women and men of deep spirituality and profound commitment to the Church.

2.   Communicating values: John MacCauley's vision

During my first five years on the Saint Meinrad development staff, I drove John MacCauley all over the state of Indiana. It was an internship that could not have been programmed. As I drove, he shared with me his understanding of development. And when there was a problem in the office, or in the wider seminary community, he would tell me about it and ask how I would handle it. He was a marvelous teacher, and in those five years he handed on to me his remarkable legacy, which he attributed to Holy Cross Father John Cavanaugh, his mentor on the development staff at the University of Notre Dame.

In this brief reflection, it's not possible for me to do justice to John MacCauley's legacy, but I would like to summarize some of the key insights that I gained from what John called his "philosophy of development."

For John MacCauley, development referred to the total process by which an institution exercises leadership, identifies its mission and goals, builds a supporting constituency around its priorities, and invites others to invest in the institution and its mission. John passionately resisted every attempt to reduce his concept of development to mere fundraising. In fact, he once said that he despised being called a fundraiser so much that it felt like someone scratching chalk on a blackboard. For John MacCauley, the techniques of fundraising were the *final and least important ingredients* in the total development process. John was convinced that articulating vision, communicating values and "telling your story" were the essential, key ingredients of a true development program. Everything else was secondary.

Looking back over three decades, I now see how important John's emphasis on *communication* was to his concept of development—especially in the context of a religious community like Saint Meinrad. Because the mission of the Church is to proclaim the Kingdom of God, and to reach out and invite all people to participate in the life of the Church, John's approach to development was not foreign to the self-understanding of the

Benedictine community (once they understood it). Using familiar Benedictine concepts like hospitality and *ora et labora* (prayer and work), John was able to design a development program that seemed to fit with the distinctive charisms of the monks of Saint Meinrad. They are not mendicants begging for alms. They are Benedictines inviting others to join in their prayer and work.

The present archabbot, the Rt. Rev. Justin Duvall, believes that the development program at Saint Meinrad was a gift of divine providence. He says that as a result of God's grace "the right people gathered at Saint Meinrad at the right time" and began a process that has sustained the community through many challenges (financial and otherwise) for the past 40 years. "The development program is a treasured gift from God," Archabbot Justin says. "Our responsibility is to be good stewards of this gift—to be grateful for it, to grow it and to share it generously with others."

The wisdom of Saint Meinrad's approach to development extends far beyond one particular religious community. I believe that a strong communications emphasis, grounded in evangelization and stewardship, is the key to integrating mission advancement into the daily life and ministry of any diocese, parish, religious community, school or other Catholic organization.

As a young development officer, I worked hard at learning from my mentor. To this day, I firmly believe that John was right. Anyone who doubts this philosophy of development should visit Saint Meinrad. During the past 40 years, many people have been responsible for Saint Meinrad's success in development. In fact, the program was never a "one-person shop." It was started more than 40 years ago with a *team*. But John MacCauley was the architect, and his vision remains the foundation for everything that is done there—even today.

As John's health declined in the early 1980s, I was asked to take charge of the development program at Saint Meinrad: first in a transitional role, and then as vice president. Looking back on those years, I believe that I accomplished two very important things.

First, I institutionalized John MacCauley's vision. Like many charismatic leaders, John was not a great administrator. Much of his knowledge remained in his head, and very few things had been established as policy or procedures. My job was to synthesize John's concept of development and to integrate it into the day-to-day operations of the institution.

The second very important thing that I did was to hire and train my successor. For 25 years, Dan Schipp did an extraordinary job of leading the development program at Saint Meinrad. He remained faithful to the founding vision, but he also moved the program forward in response to the changing needs and circumstances of the monastery and seminary communities. Dan now works as a full-time consultant sharing his wisdom and experience with others.

3. Fundraising as ministry: Father Paul Reinert, S.J.

While I was vice president for development at Saint Meinrad in the mid-1980s, I had the great privilege of working with my second mentor, Jesuit Father Paul Reinert, the former president and then chancellor of St. Louis University. For several years, Father Reinert was the chair of Saint Meinrad's development committee, and he brought to this task his special zeal for higher education and for the "ministry" of development. In fact, Father Reinert was the first person I ever heard talk about development, or fundraising, as a ministry. He believed it so strongly that he continued to play an important role in St. Louis University's major-gifts program long after he retired from his administrative responsibilities.

It was Father Reinert who taught me that this ministry called development really can make a difference in people's spiritual lives. Countless stories, which he loved to tell, showed how even stingy, lonely, self-centered people found new meaning and hope through generous sharing. When you invite people to give, Father Reinert would say, you give them an opportunity to get outside of themselves and to discover what it means to reach out to another human being in need. As development officers, we minister to people's deepest needs and highest hopes because we invite them to become a part of something important (the mission of the Church) and because we invite them to experience the joy and the freedom that comes from true generosity.

4. Teaching the joy of giving: Henry A. Rosso

In the mid-1980s, I also had the great fortune to meet, and eventually work with, Henry A. Rosso, the founder of The Fund Raising School, which is now part of the Center on Philanthropy at Indiana University. I was privileged to teach with Hank in a series of contract programs sponsored by Saint Meinrad over a three-year period for the leaders of Catholic parishes in Indiana and Kentucky.

During those years, I must have heard Hank teach the basics course (Fundraising 101) at least 50 times. But I was never bored. In fact, I always learned something new. Hank was an excellent presenter who had mastered his subject matter. His examples and his responses to questions were drawn from the vast stores of his fundraising experience. And while he frequently talked about mechanics—the nuts and bolts of fundraising practice—there was a passion, and a kind of poetry, to his teaching that was irresistible. He was a master teacher and a professional fundraiser who absolutely refused to apologize for who he was or how he earned his living!

When I first met Hank Rosso, his refusal to apologize for fundraising was incomprehensible to me. I was trained in a school of thought that regarded fundraising as mere technique. "Development" was the work of artisans; fundraising was the work of technicians. But no one could sit through 50 classes with Hank Rosso and successfully maintain that stereotype. So, under Hank's influence, I developed a much greater appreciation for the principles and techniques of professional, ethical fundraising.

The Fund Raising School is Hank Rosso's legacy, and I have been privileged to maintain an association with this remarkable institution for many years. Hank once told me that a fundraiser's primary responsibility is "to teach the joy of giving." No one lived this legacy more fully than Hank did.

5. The first decade: What I learned

Nearly 10 years into my chosen profession, I was still learning from my mentors. From them, I learned that no matter what you call it, this profession is not about money or prestige or winning campaigns. It's about the joy of giving. It's about exercising leadership and communicating values. It's about offering people opportunities to become involved in something greater than themselves. And it's not "a necessary evil" that we have to apologize for. It's a ministry. And it's a management or leadership style that is practical and that *makes a difference* in the lives of individuals and institutions.

My years as a seminary development officer at Saint Meinrad were truly years of grace and learning. Of course, there were problems and frustrations. These grand visions of development and fundraising always conflict with the realities we face every day. And, of course, there's the cynicism and skepticism that is all around us (and all too often inside us). If I had a dollar for every time in the last 40 years that I heard someone say, "Yes, but when you get right down to it, it's really all about money," I could retire a wealthy man!

What development or fundraising professionals do is really not about money. It's about the joy of giving and the privilege of asking. And anyone who plans on becoming wealthy or powerful or prestigious in this profession is in for a rude awakening! John MacCauley, Father Paul Reinert, and Hank Rosso were not wealthy men—in spite of the fact that their teaching continues to inspire thousands of people to give away hundreds of millions of dollars each year. The legacy that they left is a legacy of the heart. It cannot be measured in silver or gold.

6. Financial problems in the Catholic Church

In the late 1980s and early '90s, the Catholic Church in the U.S. was in serious financial trouble. Dioceses throughout the country were deeply in debt and were forced to close large numbers of parishes and schools in the inner city. Even small dioceses had to face the fact that expenses were growing much faster than income. Reports in the national media called attention to the Catholic Church's serious financial crises, while comparative studies on the giving habits of religious people placed Catholics near the bottom of the list of denominations.

In the context of what seemed to be a major financial crisis in the Catholic Church, Saint Meinrad's continuing success in development was a mystery (and occasionally an embarrassment). For a variety of reasons, some altruistic and some very practical, we began to explore ways that the seminary could assist neighboring dioceses in their development efforts. With the help of a series of grants from Lilly Endowment in the late 1980s, Saint Meinrad tried to share its "philosophy of development" with the larger Church.

Looking back on this effort, its amazing how ambitious (and naïve) we were. Over a three-year period, we conducted a series of programs designed to teach Catholic dioceses how to do strategic planning, how to improve communications, and how to professionalize their fundraising practice.

As with any such effort, we had a few big successes and some equally large failures, but what mainly happened was the planting of seeds. Or, as John MacCauley would say, we began to "create a climate for development." We began the gradual process of helping bishops, diocesan officials, pastors and parish leaders recognize that the old funding mechanisms had to be replaced by something completely different. It was easy enough for Catholic pastors and other church leaders to see that the old ways weren't working. But getting them to "let go" of old funding patterns and replace them with new, untested concepts and strategies was another story.

7.   The Reluctant Steward

Our recognition that clergy attitudes were both the problem and the solution led us to the research project whose findings were eventually published as *The Reluctant Steward*.

With the fervent hope that Saint Meinrad would be able to develop courses and programs to help change the way Catholic institutions raise money, we set out to explore the vast, uncharted territory of clergy attitudes about administration, finance and stewardship education in the seminary. The results of this study were significant. We discovered that most pastors (Protestant and Catholic) are deeply dissatisfied with the training they received (or failed to receive) in the seminary in the increasingly complex and frustrating areas of church administration and finance. However, if given the chance to take continuing education courses in these critical areas, they would refuse. "We were not called to be administrators, personnel directors, or fundraisers," the clergy told us.

Seminary presidents, deans and faculty showed a similar aversion to these issues. While they acknowledged that this information is vitally important to the preparation of pastors, they would much prefer that dioceses or judicatories assume this responsibility. Most seminaries don't have the experience or expertise to teach the practical techniques of church administration. They believe they already have their hands full teaching theology, liturgy, homiletics, church history and other important theological disciplines.

By the time *The Reluctant Steward* was published in 1992, I had left Saint Meinrad to become the chief development officer for the Archdiocese of Louisville. I was fascinated by the challenge of translating the successful development principles I learned at Saint Meinrad to the much more complex and decentralized environment of a Catholic diocese. I was keenly aware that what I was doing was experimental. In those days, many Catholic dioceses had a "development office," but to my knowledge at that time no diocese had anything like the comprehensive development program you would find at Saint Meinrad or at most Catholic universities.

When I arrived in the Archdiocese of Louisville, there was a planning office, a communications center, and an annual appeal office. But there was no integration or coordination of these functions—and no sense that these individual offices could ever work together in a unified way to actively promote the mission and goals of the archdiocese. I was blessed with an archbishop who listened carefully to the unfamiliar ideas I proposed and who was willing to make changes that he didn't fully understand. As a result of Archbishop Thomas C. Kelly's leadership, and the hard work of diocesan staff and volunteers, we developed a vision statement and strategic plan for the Archdiocese of Louisville. And we began to focus the communications and fundraising efforts of the archdiocese on the larger mission and goals of the local Church.

The results were more than I ever could have hoped for, and I began to see that, with some adaptation, the principles I had learned from John MacCauley, Father Paul Reinert and Hank Rosso could be successfully applied to Catholic dioceses. But, as it turned out, I had a lot more to learn.

8. The second decade: Diocesan stewardship and development

The year *The Reluctant Steward* was published (1992), the Catholic bishops of the United States published their first pastoral letter on the theology and practice of stewardship. It was called *Stewardship: A Disciple's Response* and to the dismay of many people with finance or fundraising responsibilities in the Church, it was not about church finances at all. It was about this strange "Protestant" phenomenon called stewardship.

To the best of my knowledge, I first heard the word *stewardship* at a seminary development conference in the early 1980s. It was clearly a Protestant word with no real application (I thought) to the experience of Catholics in America or anywhere else. What's more, I was aware from my colleagues' conversations that the concept of stewardship was not universally understood or accepted even among Protestants. So it was a very strange experience to hear Catholic bishops promoting the concept of stewardship as "the solution" to the urgent financial problems facing the Church in the United States.

My first reaction was negative. We don't need stewardship, I thought. We need development—understood as effective leadership and planning, excellent communications, and professional, ethical fundraising. I feared that the Catholic bishops, like the Protestant and Catholic clergy we surveyed for *The Reluctant Steward*, were simply afraid to face financial realities and were hiding behind some quasi-religious concepts borrowed from other Christian denominations.

9. What do I own and what owns me: Archbishop Thomas J. Murphy

Then I met Seattle Archbishop Thomas J. Murphy, who chaired the bishops' ad hoc committee on stewardship and who was the principal architect of their pastoral letter, *Stewardship: A Disciple's Response.* I had the great privilege of teaching with Archbishop Murphy in the International Catholic Stewardship Council's summer institute, and with the archbishop's help, I began to see that the concept of stewardship has important things to say to individual Catholics and to the Church as a whole.

In their pastoral letter, the bishops talk about stewardship as a mature form of discipleship, the way a follower of Jesus Christ lives concretely and practically in the world. Stewardship, they say, is an attitude of the mind and heart that expresses itself in action. It is not a program or a series of actions. The bishops describe "a Christian steward" as someone who is grateful, generous, accountable, and willing to return God's gifts with increase. In their view, a mature commitment to stewardship changes the way we live—and think. And teaching stewardship as a way of life means helping people experience the joys of giving and sharing—without counting the cost, out of a profound sense of justice and charity.

This was Archbishop Murphy's vision. In fact, it was his passion and one of the driving forces of his life. In the five years between the publication of the stewardship pastoral in 1992 and his untimely death in 1997,

Archbishop Murphy traveled all over North America giving talks on stewardship. It was not unusual for him to schedule these talks on a Tuesday (his day off) so that he could take "a red-eye" flight from Seattle on Monday night, fly to Dallas, Orlando or Boston to give his stewardship talk, and then return home Tuesday night so that he could be back in his archdiocese on Wednesday morning.

I started out being skeptical about stewardship as the solution to the Church's financial problems, and I still caution against using the spirituality of stewardship as an excuse for avoiding important fiscal realities; but I now firmly believe in stewardship as a way of life, and I proudly consider myself to be a disciple of Archbishop Murphy. He had a keen insight into human nature, and he was a passionate advocate for the power of stewardship to transform people's experience of daily life. I believe that we Catholics owe an immense debt of gratitude to Archbishop Murphy. Without his personal witness to stewardship—and his leadership in the drafting of the pastoral letter—it would be *much harder* for parish and diocesan leaders in the Catholic Church to teach the joy of giving and to feel privileged in the ministry of asking!

10. Planning, communications and development: The Archdiocese of Louisville

For six years (during the late 1980s and early 1990s), I served the Catholic Archdiocese of Louisville as executive director of the Office of Planning and Development and as chief communications officer. During this time, we integrated planning, communications, and fundraising into the overall management style of the archdiocese, and we began a stewardship education program that involved every parish in the archdiocese.

During the same period, I served as a planning consultant to several other dioceses and religious organizations primarily in the Midwest and South. I was convinced that the discipline of planning could help church-related organizations become better stewards of the human, physical and financial resources entrusted to their care. I also believed that good planning, and much better communications, would help the Church address successfully the financial problems that seemed especially threatening a decade ago.

The Archdiocese of Louisville also launched my career as a stewardship writer. In 1988, I began to write a weekly column on stewardship themes called "The Good Steward." At first, I was afraid that I might quickly run out of things to say. But it didn't take long for me to realize that if stewardship really is a way of living the Gospel, we will never run out of things to talk about. All of life's challenges and opportunities have a stewardship dimension, and after more than 20 years of writing articles and books on stewardship, the aim of my writing is still to offer a stewardship perspective on the experiences of daily Christian living.

I am deeply indebted to Archbishop Kelly for the gifts he shared with me during my years of service to the Church in central Kentucky. The good work we began in the late 1980s, has been continued with great success by Archbishop Joseph Kurtz, Dr. Brian Reynolds, and many others—culminating in the 200th anniversary of the founding of this local Church as the Diocese of Bardstown in 1808, and a historic capital campaign, *Building a Future of Hope!*

11. A Legacy of Hope: The Archdiocese of Indianapolis

In 1993, I was given a unique opportunity to test my skills as a development officer. For the eight years that I served on the development staff at Saint Meinrad, the president-rector of our School of Theology was Father Daniel Buechlein, a Benedictine monk who taught me philosophy and theology when I was in the seminary. He is a deeply spiritual man who is also a remarkably gifted administrator. (His unique gifts and talents were recognized very early in his life. He became president-rector at Saint Meinrad School of Theology when he was 33 years old!) After 17 years as a seminary president, Father Daniel was named bishop of Memphis by Pope John Paul II in 1987. Five years later, he was appointed Archbishop of Indianapolis.

At Archbishop Daniel's invitation, I joined the diocesan staff in Indianapolis as secretary for planning, communications and development. The five years that I spent in Indianapolis represent a virtual "textbook case" in development. First, we drafted a strategic plan for the archdiocese and a series of satellite plans for various agencies and institutions in the archdiocese. Then we substantially improved archdiocesan communications both internally and among external publics. And, last but certainly not least, we professionalized the archdiocese's fundraising programs—in the context of a parish-based stewardship education program and the first comprehensive capital campaign in the archdiocese's history.

Looking back over that five-year period from 1993 to 1998, it's easy to see that the Indianapolis archdiocese was ready for the changes that we introduced. And, of course, some changes happened more smoothly and effectively than others. But there is no question that the philosophy of development that Archbishop Daniel and I learned together at Saint Meinrad made a substantial difference in our ability to teach stewardship as a way of life and to develop the resources that are needed to carry out the Church's mission. In fact, my experiences in Indianapolis convinced me beyond any doubt that *it is possible* for a Catholic diocese to integrate the functions of planning, communications and fundraising into a comprehensive development or mission-advancement program. It's possible, but it's not easy. And the larger the diocese, the harder it is to coordinate these functions and direct them in ways that further the Church's long-term mission and goals.

Early in his tenure as archbishop of Indianapolis, Archbishop Buechlein recognized the need for a major fundraising campaign for long overdue capital projects in parishes and in the archdiocese. The initiatives we had undertaken in the areas of planning, communications, stewardship education and development were beginning to take root, and in 1997 (five years after Archbishop Buechlein arrived in Indianapolis) we began to prepare for the first archdiocesan-wide capital campaign in the history of the Church in central and southern Indiana.

In spite of our strong development staff, and the growth we were experiencing in all facets of our advancement program, we recognized the importance of retaining a professional fundraising firm to guide our overall efforts and direct campaigns in all 150 parishes. As we looked for counsel, we identified three requirements:

- A successful track record—especially in major-gift development
- The ability to reinforce principles of Christian stewardship
- Flexibility and the ability to collaborate with archdiocesan and parish leaders.

As the result of a complex process involving many people, including development officers from other dioceses that had recently conducted capital campaigns, we chose Resources Services Incorporated (RSI).

RSI was founded by two Protestant ministers in the mid 1970s. Their objective was to bring a biblical stewardship perspective to church fundraising. In the early years, RSI worked mainly with Protestant churches in the south, but the firm quickly expanded its scope to include churches in all regions of the United States. In the mid 1990s, following the publication of the U.S. bishops' pastoral letter on stewardship, Catholic parishes and dioceses naturally turned to RSI to help them introduce stewardship principles into their fundraising programs.

In the first Indianapolis campaign, which we called A Legacy of Hope: From Generation to Generation, RSI provided counsel for the archdiocesan major-gifts campaign and for a groundbreaking effort to raise money from local corporations and foundations for Catholic schools and social services in the center city. RSI also conducted individual stewardship-based campaigns in each of the archdiocese's 150 parishes. The collaboration between the Archdiocese of Indianapolis and RSI in the Legacy of Hope campaign was a particularly successful one from several perspectives. The archdiocese's minimum campaign goal of $40 million was exceeded by more than double for a total of $87 million. Parishes and schools throughout central and southern Indiana received funding to meet urgent growth and deferred maintenance needs. And, most importantly, the sound platform established for archdiocesan development efforts, and for teaching the spirituality of stewardship, was enhanced in the process.

During the past 16 years, the Archdiocese of Indianapolis has raised more than $300 million, over and above weekly parish income, to support archdiocesan shared ministries and the capital and endowment needs of parishes, schools and archdiocesan agencies. In the archdiocese's most recent campaign, which raised more than $114 million, more than 14,000 people were actively engaged in the process. The "experiment" of mission advancement is clearly succeeding in the Archdiocese of Indianapolis— thanks to the leadership and hard work of Archbishop Buechlein and many dedicated clergy and lay leaders!

12. Sharing Christ's Gifts: The Archdiocese of Chicago

In 1998, I began working for the Archdiocese of Chicago, the second largest diocese in the United States, with 2.3 million Catholics and 378 parishes in two counties of northeastern Illinois. The Archdiocese of Chicago has enormous development potential. It is a vibrant local Church with a rich history and a tradition of strong faith. I accepted the challenge of working in the Archdiocese of Chicago for two main reasons: First, to help Cardinal Francis George teach stewardship as a way of life. And, second, to begin a long-term process designed to professionalize the archdiocese's fundraising practice.

For personal and family reasons, I was not able to remain in Chicago for more than 18 months, but during my time there we initiated some things that are clearly making a difference. First, with Cardinal George's leadership and support, we made a commitment to stewardship education. Although Archbishop Murphy had died the year before, we brought his stewardship message home to his native Chicago on videotape through a series of presentations in all of the archdiocese's vicariates.

Second, we launched the first archdiocesan capital campaign in more than 40 years and raised more than $240 million on a $200 million goal. The Archdiocese of Chicago's millennium campaign, *Sharing Christ's Gifts,* was a stewardship-based effort that provided significant resources to each participating parish and that demonstrated the unity and solidarity of the Church in Cook and Lake counties.

Finally, we developed initiatives that have resulted in the gradual professionalization and growth of the archdiocese's development efforts including the Annual Catholic Appeal, major and planned gifts, and the ongoing capital and endowment needs of parishes, schools and other Catholic organizations in the Archdiocese of Chicago.

Cardinal George is first and foremost a bishop, a spiritual leader who cares deeply about the pastoral needs of his priests and the people of his diocese. As a result of the cardinal's leadership, stewardship and evangelization became the centerpieces of the archdiocese's millennium campaign, and they have continued to be dominant themes in the life of this local Church ever since.

In 1998, a Chicago pastor told me, "We don't do stewardship here. When we need money, we shake the tree. When we need more, we shake it harder." Ten years later, this attitude has changed significantly, and stewardship is truly becoming a way of life in this great archdiocese!

13. The third decade: Teaching, writing and consulting

In October 1999, I was invited to join the staff of RSI to help create a division that would be exclusively devoted to serving the stewardship education and capital fundraising needs of Catholic dioceses. After more than eight years with RSI, the division I helped to create, RSI Catholic Services, was acquired by a firm which specializes in financial consulting for Catholic dioceses and religious communities. Now under the name O'Meara, Ferguson, Whelan and Conway, Inc. (O'Meara Ferguson), we offer a distinctive, integrated approach to helping the Church develop the temporal resources needed to carry out Christ's work.

O'Meara Ferguson's mission is "to provide Catholic organizations with advice and counsel on the best possible use of their temporal resources as they work to further their missions." The firm "integrates specifically crafted financial strategies, unmatched access to capital financing alternatives, investment management advice and tested development counsel to manage and leverage financial assets to build our clients' fiscal strength and independence." It is an ambitious undertaking—especially in an increasingly uncertain economic climate, but with the help of God's grace, we are making a difference in the way Catholic organizations manage and develop the Church's temporal resources!

I have been privileged to serve the Church as a full-time teacher, writer and consultant for more than nine years now, and in the process I have developed strong friendships with bishops and diocesan officials in more than 30 dioceses in all regions of the United States. As Archbishop Murphy used to say, the geographic, economic and cultural diversity of the Church in the United States is a great blessing, but it also challenges us to adapt to the distinctive needs and circumstances of the people we serve. Stewardship principles are the same in Indiana and New Mexico, for example, but how we teach these principles, and encourage their practice, must reflect a keen sense of the particular place and its people.

During my years as a consultant, there have been many obstacles facing the Church in the United States. Scandals, economic downturns and terrorist attacks caused bishops, pastors and the Catholic people to be preoccupied with immediate problems rather than new opportunities.

In those years, the climate for mission advancement suffered setbacks. Interestingly, the large-scale defections that were predicted by many media pundits in the wake of the clergy sex-abuse scandal never materialized. Catholics continued to give generously—especially at the parish level. But Church leaders were clearly distracted and most were unwilling to take the kinds of risks that are required to invest in mission advancement. During the height of the scandal, many dioceses cancelled plans for capital campaigns. Others discontinued, or low-keyed, their ongoing fundraising efforts—fearing that donors would hesitate to give to dioceses that were subject to increasing lawsuits and attorneys' fees. It was a tough time for all.

And yet, there were many successes. Diocesan capital campaigns that we helped to conduct in Chicago, Erie, Green Bay, Indianapolis, Knoxville, Lubbock (Texas), Sioux Falls and Wilmington exceeded their goals (sometimes dramatically). Stewardship education efforts were launched in Brooklyn, Cleveland, Indianapolis, Los Angeles, Pittsburgh, Orlando, and San Bernardino. Strategic plans were developed in New Orleans, Springfield in Illinois, St. Louis, and St. Cloud (Minnesota). During this period, we provided stewardship-based fundraising counsel to more than 1,000 parishes, schools and other Catholic organizations throughout many different regions of the United States.

I believe that the stewardship movement in the United States, Canada, Australia and many other parts of the world has flourished during the past decade—in spite of many obstacles—because of the efforts of clergy and lay leaders who have taken the spirituality of stewardship to heart. At the same time, I think that mission advancement, understood as a process designed to professionalize the Church's approach to resource development, or fundraising, has been slowed down by the aftereffects of scandal and economic uncertainty. Catholic higher education and Catholic health care have been able to embrace principles of advancement and to integrate them into the business of being a Catholic university or hospital. The same cannot be said of most dioceses and religious orders. There is still too much of a disconnect between the self-understanding of religious institutions and the practice of professional fundraising for most to embrace development or mission advancement as integral to their daily life or functioning.

The question that is frequently asked by bishops, pastors, religious superiors and the leaders of Catholic organizations that do not have fully functioning development programs is "Why do wealthy Catholics give generously to colleges and universities, to health care institutions, to arts organizations and other causes but not to the Church?" Why indeed?

Based on my experience during the past three decades, I believe the answer is simple, but not easy. Simply stated, in most cases the Church has not made the kind of commitment that is needed to plan and implement a comprehensive mission-advancement program. What is required is clear vision, engaged leadership, excellent communications and a disciplined and professional approach to the overall fundraising process. Why hasn't the Church made this commitment? That is much harder to explain—and to overcome.

The good news is that we are making progress. Stewardship has taken root and is growing. Mission advancement, while still lagging behind the experiences of secular institutions and many individual Catholic organizations (especially higher education and health care), is on the rise. Several dioceses have made significant investments in planning, communications and professional fundraising. As John MacCauley would say, we are gradually "creating a climate for development" in the Church. May the Lord, who has begun this good work in and through us, now bring it to completion.

14. The decade(s) ahead: Advancing the mission of the Church

As I noted in the foreword to this book of reflections, after more than three decades, I know that my professional calling—my life's work—is to help the Church integrate principles of Christian stewardship with the practice of professional fundraising.

The means to this end is mission advancement, a series of processes or techniques that can help bishops, pastors, religious superiors and other Church leaders develop the resources they need to advance the Church's mission and, in so doing, to continue Christ's work of teaching, healing and sanctifying all God's people here and now.

It's my hope that these personal reflections—my mission advancement story—will help others understand why this work is vital to carrying out the mission of the Church. I believe that mission advancement, which includes stewardship, development and fundraising, is at the heart of the Church's mission. Properly understood and carried out, the work of mission advancement is closely linked to evangelization and to the ministry of charity. Mission advancement invites, and challenges, people of faith to acknowledge their giftedness and to share with others, gratefully and generously, from the fullness of God's bounty. This requires Church leaders to communicate clearly and persuasively how God has blessed us with spiritual and material gifts; how the Lord invites us to develop and grow all these gifts; and how our sacrificial gifts of time, talent and treasure really do make a difference in the lives of others. Mission advancement also requires that Church leaders ask members of the Catholic community boldly and unselfconsciously to "give back to the Lord with increase" without counting the cost to themselves.

God willing, I would like to continue teaching, writing and consulting in the field of mission advancement for many years to come. *That in all things God may be glorified through Jesus Christ, to whom belong glory and dominion forever and ever. Amen* (1 Pt 4:11).

Daniel Conway

❧ Prayer ☙

Lord Jesus Christ, you are the meaning of the world and of human life. You are the goal of all our desires, the satisfaction of all our longings, and the end of all our work.

Help us seek and find you in all that we do. May we be faithful disciples and responsible stewards of all your gifts.

Lord, by the power of your grace, fill our hearts with lasting joy and make us one with you now and in the world to come. Amen.

Stewards of Mission

The Church is missionary by its very nature, and Christians, disciples of Jesus Christ, are called to be stewards of the Church's mission.

This very special form of stewardship is what makes "mission advancement" much more than a series of techniques for recruiting volunteers or raising financial resources to carry out the Church's ministries. We do not apologize for undertaking these very necessary, practical functions of planning, communications and fundraising, but we understand them in a broader context, and we refuse to let them become "the tail that wags the dog."

Because we are stewards of the Church's mission, we understand our work to be a participation in the threefold ministry of the apostles, and their successors, to sanctify, to teach and to govern the People of God. In the Church, mission advancement is intended to provide leadership and support for the sacramental and pastoral ministries of the Christian community, for lifelong faith formation, and for the ministry of charity. As noted frequently in the essays contained in this little book of reflections, mission advancement is a means to an end, not an end in itself.

As our Holy Father Pope John Paul II reminded us in his Apostolic Letter, *Novo Millennio Ineunte,* the planning that we are called to do in mission advancement "is not a matter of inventing a new program. The program already exists. It is the plan founded in the Gospel and in the living Tradition, it is the same as ever. Ultimately it has its center in Christ himself, who is known, loved and imitated, so that in him we may have the life of the Trinity, and with him transform history until its fulfillment in the heavenly Jerusalem."

In the Church, planning, communications and fundraising, the three-legged stool that is mission advancement, must find its center in the person of Jesus Christ. And its ultimate goal must be to transform individuals and organizations according to the program that already exists in the Gospel and in the living Tradition of the Church.

That in all things God may be glorified.